Fodor's
25 Best

PARIS

1/20

Contents

KEY TO SYMBOLS

➕ Map reference to the accompanying pull-out map

✉ Address

☎ Telephone number

🕐 Opening/closing times

🍴 Restaurant or café

Ⓜ Nearest Métro (subway) station

🚌 Nearest bus route

🚆 Nearest rail station

ENTERTAINMENT 130

Whether you're after a cultural fix or just want a place to relax with a drink after a hard day's sight-seeing, we've made the best choices for you.

EAT 140

Uncover great dining experiences, from a quick bite at lunch to top-notch evening meals.

SLEEP 152

We've brought together the best hotels in the city, whatever budget you're on.

NEED TO KNOW 160

The practical information you need to make your trip run smoothly.

PULL-OUT MAP

The pull-out map with this book is a comprehensive street plan of the city. We've given grid references within the book for each sight and listing.

🚢 Nearest riverboat or ferry stop
♿ Facilities for visitors with disabilities
🛈 Tourist information
❓ Other practical information

🎟 Admission charges: Expensive (over €12), Moderate (€6–€12) and Inexpensive (under €6)
▷ Further information

Introducing Paris

The City of Light needs no introduction: the Eiffel Tower, Sacré-Cœur, the Louvre. It is not a museum, however, but a vibrant urban area. The monuments won't change, but everything else will. Forget stereotypes and see the city with new eyes.

Paris has been making a concerted effort to change its image as a cold city full of rude, arrogant people. That reputation was never entirely deserved, but the good news for both visitors and residents is that Paris has undergone many changes for the better. The mayor's office and the national government sponsor a number of popular (and free) annual events along the lines of the *Fête de la Musique* (21 June), which bring the normally reserved Parisians out to have fun.

In addition to *Paris Plages*, when the Right Bank of the Seine becomes a sandy beach for one month in the summer, the city is the site of *La Nuit des Musées* (May), when several museums stay open all night; *Les Journées du Patrimoine* (September), when normally off-limits monuments are open; *La Nuit Blanche* (October), for all-night art and cultural events; and outdoor music concerts in the summer.

And Paris is no longer deserted in August. At one time it became a quiet village while the working population holidayed elsewhere, but the French have now learned to stagger their holidays. Paris in August is still quiet, but more and more restaurants and shops are open. Picnicking in the city is now popular and the banks of the Seine and parks are full of outdoor diners. The once-forbidden lawns in its parks and squares are packed with children and sunbathers enjoying the summer sun.

Most visitors come to see the great monuments, however. Having miraculously survived wars and revolution—some of them for a thousand years—they now seem to be eternal.

In recent years, much effort has gone into improving the quality of life in Paris, with projects like the Vélib' bicycle hire scheme (▷ 167) and *Paris Plages* enjoyed by Parisians and visitors alike.

FACTS AND FIGURES

- Population: 2.2 million
- Area: 105 sq km (40.5 sq miles)
- GDP (Île de France): 26 percent of the country's total GDP
- Highest spot: Montmartre (128m/420ft)
- Mayor: Anne Hildago (Socialist)
- Divided into 20 *arrondissements*
- Eiffel Tower: The tower has 2.5 million rivets and is lit by 20,000 light bulbs

FLIGHT OF FANCY

The first manned flight took place in Paris when Pilatre de Rozier and the Marquis d'Arlandes made a 25-minute trip in a hot-air balloon from the Bois de Boulogne to what is now the 13th *arrondissement* on 21 November 1783. Among the crowd observing their feat was none other than Benjamin Franklin, one of the founding fathers of the USA.

CLOSED

Every Tuesday a crowd of disappointed tourists gathers outside the closed entrance to the Louvre pyramid. Remember that most major museums are closed one day a week: Monday for the city-run museums (such as the Musée Carnavalet and Musée d'Art Moderne de la Ville de Paris) and Tuesday for national museums (including the Louvre, Centre Pompidou and Grand Palais).

DID YOU KNOW?

● Every evening, nearly 300 Parisian monuments, hotels, churches, fountains, bridges and canals are illuminated against the night sky.
● France has banned smoking inside restaurants, bars and cafés, for the dining pleasure of all.
● Watch your step! In spite of the city's best efforts to alleviate the problem, dog droppings are still a hazard.

5

Focus On Paris On Screen

Few places are as closely associated with the film industry as Paris, the birthplace of cinema and a city whose many charms have been embedded in the world's imagination through the movies.

Birth of a New Medium

The history of modern cinema began properly in Paris on 28 December 1895, in the Salon Indien of the Grand Café on the boulevard des Capucines. At this venue, the Lumière brothers, Louis and Auguste, first demonstrated the potential of their invention, the *cinématographe*—a portable camera, film processing unit and projector combined—by screening 10 of their short films to a paying audience. The first film they showed was *La Sortie des Usines Lumière*, a simple shot of workers leaving the family's factory in Lyon. It lasted less than a minute, yet the public response was immediate and enthusiastic. A new entertainment medium had hit the scene, paving the way for one of the most influential and commercial entertainment genres for future generations.

The Parisian Scene

Throughout cinema history, Paris itself has been one of the great stars of the silver screen. In the 1926 silent film *Paris*, Charles Ray fell for Joan Crawford in the louche setting of the Paris Apache (pronounced Ah-Pahsh) or demi-monde, the era of hedonistic lifestyles and decadent jazz clubs. The Apaches were originally Paris members of street gangs, and later the name was used for a new dance. In the 1950s, a string of big-budget Hollywood movies, from *An American in Paris* (1951) to *Funny Face* (1957), peddled the image of Paris as the capital of love and romance to a receptive international audience, with gamine European actresses like Leslie Caron and Audrey

Clockwise from top: La Pagode cinema in rue de Babylone; Le Champo cinema in rue des Écoles; a scene from An American in Paris, *1951;* Amélie *was*

Hepburn personifying its elegance and fashion sense. In *Sabrina* (1954), Hepburn can be seen composing a letter to the wistful tune of "La Vie en Rose" as the Sacré-Cœur is seen through an open window. The film and its content may only ever have been an outsider's ideal of the City of Light, but as myths go it was a potent one. Hepburn was a Parisian *ingénue* in *Love in the Afternoon* (1957) and returned for *Paris When It Sizzles* (1964), though by then, perhaps, the formula had become a little stale.

Beyond the Romance
Inevitably, the depiction of Paris in French cinema has been somewhat less starry-eyed. Jean-Luc Godard's *Breathless* (*À bout de souffle*; 1960) may have had the relationship between Jean-Paul Belmondo and Jean Seberg at its core, but this *nouvelle vague* masterpiece is no sugar-coated romance. François Truffaut's *The Last Metro* (1980) dealt with the perils of the German occupation, Cyril Collard's *Savage Nights* (1992) with the complications of love in a time of AIDS. But French cinema is not immune to the capital's charms either, as Jean-Pierre Jeunet's magical, color-saturated *Amélie* (2001) proved to huge international success. The film featured Audrey Tautou as a shy waitress in a Montmartre café and Paris itself—as enchanting as in any 1950s musical—was her co-star.

The Tradition Maintained
Paris has remained true to its early passion for film. Director Luc Besson's project for La Cité du Cinéma (City of Cinema), which opened in 2012, has brought 45,000 sq m (484,400 sq ft) of film production space to a former power station in the northern suburb of Saint-Denis. The impact of film on the city comes full circle.

filmed at the Les Deux Moulins café; a poster for the Lumière brothers' new world of cinema; at work on Paris When it Sizzles, *1964*

Top Tips For...

These great suggestions will help you tailor your ideal visit to Paris, no matter how you choose to spend your time. Each sight or listing has a fuller write-up elsewhere in the book.

Antiquing

Hunt for a bargain at the **Marché aux Puces de Saint-Ouen** (▷ 28–29), an immense weekend flea market.

Put in a bid for the unique items at **Drouot Richelieu auction house** (▷ 125).

Browse the vintage bookstores in **Passage Verdeau** (▷ 20–21).

Haute Couture

Explore the creative process at **Musée Yves Saint Laurent** (▷ 72).

Find a wide selection of designer clothing at the department stores **Le Bon Marché Rive Gauche** (▷ 124), **Galeries Lafayette** or **Printemps** (▷ 126, panel).

Shop at the global headquarters of iconic French labels **Dior** on avenue Montaigne (▷ 125) and **Cartier** at rue de la Paix (▷ 124).

Fine Dining

Check out the Michelin-starred **Gordon Ramsay au Trianon** (▷ 148), a luxurious dining experience on a trip to Versailles.

Find out how **Guy Savoy** turns cooking into an art form at his eponymous restaurant (▷ 148–149).

Put yourself in the hands of chef Eric Frechon and try his tasting menu at **Epicure** (▷ 148).

All-Night Antics

Drink martinis into the wee hours in the old-fashioned New World ambience of **Harry's New York Bar** (▷ 137).

Gasp at the high-kicking routines at **Le Crazy Horse** cabaret show (▷ 136).

Clockwise from top: A market stall at the Marché aux Puces de Saint-Ouen; relaxing in the Jardin du Luxembourg; an art installation at Musée d'Art Moderne

Descend into the medieval basement at **Caveau de la Huchette** for jazz (▷ 135). Take in a concert at the **Divan du Monde** (▷ 137) and afterwards hear some guest DJs.

Catering to the Kids
Ride the glass elevator to the top of the **Eiffel Tower** (▷ 60–61).
Explore interactive exhibitions at the **Cité des Sciences et de l'Industrie** (▷ 76).
Set the little darlings loose in the **Si Tu Veux** toy shop (▷ 129).
See a dinosaur skeleton at the **Muséum National d'Histoire Naturelle** (▷ 72).

Shoestring Pleasures
Take advantage of free admission to the permanent collections of all city-run museums: the **Maison de Victor Hugo** at place des Vosges (▷ 53), **Musée d'Art Moderne de la Ville de Paris** (▷ 69) and many more.
Visit the **Atelier Brancusi**, a reconstruction of sculptor Constantin Brancusi's workshop, in front of the **Centre Georges Pompidou** (▷ 16–17), for free.

Bird's-Eye Views
Check out the view from **Printemps de la Maison's** ninth floor (▷ 126, panel).
Take in the view from the terrace of **La Grande Arche** at **La Défense** (▷ 76).
Eat in the Eiffel Tower's **Le Jules Verne** restaurant (▷ 149) for fine food with views.

Lazy Mornings
Cruise leisurely down the Seine in a *bateau mouche* (▷ 58–59).
Commune with the ghosts of Sartre and Hemingway at the **Café de Flore** (▷ 66).
Sit by the fountain in the **Domaine Nationale du Palais Royal** (▷ 66–67) with a book by Colette, who once lived there.

de la Ville de Paris; Harry's New York Bar in rue Daunou; the impressive glass dome of the prestigious Galeries Lafayette department store

Timeline

BEFORE 1000

- The Celtic tribe of Parisii settles on Île de la Cité around 200 BC.
- By AD 100 the Roman city of Lutetia, later Paris, is growing fast.
- In 451 Sainte Geneviève saves Paris from the threat of Attila the Hun.

1163 The building of Notre-Dame starts.

1337–1453 Hundred Years' War between France and England.

1431 Henry VI of England is crowned king of France in Notre-Dame.

1437 Charles VII regains control of Paris.

1572 St. Bartholomew Massacre occurs during the Wars of Religion.

1682 Louis XIV and the court move to Versailles.

1700s Intellectuals, including Rousseau and Diderot, introduce radical new ideas during the Age of Enlightenment.

1789 Storming of the Bastille.

1792 Monarchy abolished; proclamation of the Republic.

1804 Napoleon crowned emperor.

1830 Bourbons overthrown; Louis-Philippe crowned.

1848 Revolution topples Louis-Philippe; Second Republic headed by Napoleon III, who is later crowned emperor.

REIGN OF TERROR

From 1793 to 1794 the Reign of Terror seized France, masterminded by the ruthless, power-crazed Jacobin leaders Maximilien Robespierre and Georges Jacques Danton. The king, Louis XVI, was convicted of treason and guillotined in January 1793, followed in October by his queen, Marie-Antoinette. By mid-1794 more than 18,000 people are estimated to have been beheaded in France.

The gardens at the Château de Versailles

The Consecration of the Emperor Napoleon, by Jacques-Louis David

1852–70 Baron Haussmann oversees the transformation of Paris.

1870–71 Paris besieged by Prussians, civil uprising of the Commune, Republic restored.

1889 Eiffel Tower is completed.

1900 First Métro line opens.

1914–18 Paris bombarded by German cannon.

1940 Nazis occupy Paris, followed by Liberation in 1944.

1958 De Gaulle heads Fifth Republic.

1977 Jacques Chirac is elected mayor (then president in 1995). Centre Georges Pompidou opens.

1981 Election of President Mitterrand. He initiates his *Grands Projets*—a new building scheme.

2002 First *Paris Plage*, in which riverside roads are closed in summer to create an urban beach on the banks of the Seine.

2014 Anne Hidalgo is elected the first female mayor of the city.

2015 Terrorist attacks shock the city, but 1.6 million people march through Paris in defense of liberty.

2016 France hosts Euro 2016 football tournament, holding the final in Paris.

2019 Notre-Dame is partially destroyed by a major fire, with the roof and spire collapsing.

The Liberation of Paris, 1944

THE SEINE

The city's history has been inextricably linked with the River Seine since its earliest origins as a Gaulish village on the Île de la Cité, an islet in the river. The Seine represents the very lifeblood of Paris, flowing majestically through its heart, animating the city, defining the capital geographically and reflecting its history in the many fine buildings that line its banks. After centuries of pollution—when the river was used as a sewer—the Seine has been cleaned and its water is less polluted than it has been for years, although it's probably not a good idea to jump in for a swim.

★ Top 25

This section contains the must-see Top 25 sights and experiences in Paris. They are listed alphabetically, and numbered so you can locate them on the inside front cover.

TOP 25

HIGHLIGHTS

● Views from the terrace
● *La Marseillaise*, François Rude
● Tomb of the Unknown Soldier

TIP

● The museum has audio-visual displays illustrating major historical events and the construction of the Arc.

At the hub of Haussmann's web of 12 avenues, which reach out like tentacles towards the city beyond, this is the ultimate symbol of Napoleon's military pretensions and might. Climb the 284 steps to the terrace for superb views.

National symbol Napoleon conceived the Arc de Triomphe as a symbol of his military might in 1806 but it was finished only in 1836 by Louis-Philippe. Two centuries on and the colossal monument is still an iconic image of national pride. It plays a central role in many of France's key commemorations, including VE Day (8 May), Bastille Day (14 July) and Remembrance Day (11 November). Within its grounds are the Tomb of the Unknown Soldier, installed in 1921 after World War I, and a

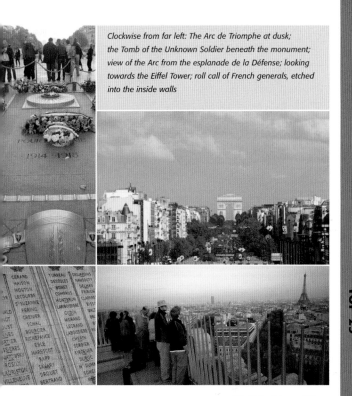

Clockwise from far left: The Arc de Triomphe at dusk; the Tomb of the Unknown Soldier beneath the monument; view of the Arc from the esplanade de la Défense; looking towards the Eiffel Tower; roll call of French generals, etched into the inside walls

poignant Memorial Flame, added two years later. This flame is rekindled every evening.

Special interest There are wonderful views from the rooftop, 50m (164ft) high. From here you can admire Haussmann's weblike street design and look along the Grand Axis toward place de la Concorde in one direction and the Grande Arche in the other. There is a small shop and museum on the way up. At ground level, admire the magnificent sculpted facade, the work of three artists. Don't miss the winged figure of Liberty on François Rude's sculpture *La Marseillaise*, calling the French to defend their nation (northeastern pillar, facing the Champs-Élysées). The 30 shields studding the crown of the arch each bear the name of a Revolutionary or Imperial victory.

THE BASICS

paris-arc-de-triomphe.fr

B2

Place Charles-de-Gaulle, 75008

01 55 37 73 77

Apr–Sep daily 10am–11pm; Oct–Mar 10am–10.30pm. Times may vary. Last admission 45 mins before closing

Charles de Gaulle–Étoile

22, 30, 31, 52, 73, 92

Moderate

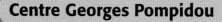

HIGHLIGHTS

● Design by Sir Richard Rogers, Renzo Piano and Jean-François Bodin
● View from the escalator
● Stravinsky fountain
● Stylish design in Georges restaurant
● *Avant-premières* (promotional events) for new and existing work of many top cinema directors
● Design shop on level 1

TIP

● Lines for tickets can be long; cut waiting times by booking in advance online.

Late opening hours make an exhibition visit possible between an *apéritif* and dinner in this controversial cultural area. Take your pick between the genesis of modernism, an art film or a drama performance.

High-tech culture More than a mere landmark in the extensive face-lift that Paris has undergone since the 1970s, the high-tech Centre Pompidou (known to Parisians as Beaubourg) is a hive of changing cultural activity. Contemporary art, architecture, design, photography, theater, cinema and dance are all represented, while the lofty structure offers exceptional views over central Paris. Take the transparent escalator tubes for a bird's-eye view of the piazza, where jugglers, artists, musicians and portrait artists perform for the crowds.

Clockwise from far left: The inside-out exterior of the building; detail of the Stravinsky fountain outside the Centre; futuristic features on the exterior; glass corridor with fine views over the city; the Centre viewed above the rooftops of the city; more pipes and structures on the facade

Classic modernism The Musée National d'Art Moderne's permanent collections feature work from 1905 to the 1960s on the fifth floor, with works from the contemporary collection on level four. Items displayed from the 59,000-strong collection change regularly and range from cubism by Georges Braque to Pop Art by Andy Warhol and video art by Korean artist Nam June Paik. For a chronological overview start on the fifth floor. Levels 1, 4 and 6 hold temporary exhibitions, while an information library is on levels 1, 2 and 3. The ground level includes a bookshop and museum boutique (there are other bookstands located on levels 4 and 6), a post office and a children's workshop. There are cinemas on the first and lower floors, and the restaurant Georges, with its wonderful views over the city, is on the top floor.

THE BASICS

centrepompidou.fr

➕ K5

✉ Place Georges-Pompidou, 75004

☎ 01 44 78 12 33

🕐 Museum and exhibits Wed–Mon 11–9. Last tickets 8. Atelier Brancusi (▷ 9) Wed–Mon 2–6. Library Mon, Wed–Fri 12–10, Sat–Sun 11–10

🍴 Georges restaurant on 6th floor; café

🚇 Rambuteau, Hôtel de Ville

🚌 29, 38, 39, 47, 58, 67, 75, 76, 81

🚈 RER Line A, B, Châtelet–Les Halles

♿ Excellent

💷 Expensive

HIGHLIGHTS

- Marie-Antoinette's cell
- Tour Bonbec
- Prisoners' cells upstairs

TIP

- If you also plan to visit Sainte-Chapelle (▷ 56–57), go to the Conciergerie first and buy a joint ticket, to avoid the lines at Sainte-Chapelle. But do try to get to Sainte-Chapelle in the morning, before it gets very busy.

The ghosts of the victims of the guillotine must surely haunt this stark and gloomy place that served as a prison and torture chamber for more than five centuries. It remains full of macabre mementoes of its grisly past.

From palace to prison Rising over the Seine in menacing grandeur, the Conciergerie was built from 1299 to 1313 as part of a royal complex that also included Sainte-Chapelle. From 1391 until 1914 the building functioned as a prison and torture chamber, its reputation striking fear in the population. During the Revolution more than 2,700 people appeared before the Revolutionary Tribunal at the Conciergerie, including Marie-Antoinette and Maximilien Robespierre.

Clockwise from top left: The beautiful Conciergerie graces the banks of the Seine; detail of the building flanked by trees; the impressive clock on the Tour de l'Horloge; representation of the clerk's room; the moody lighting enhances the Salle des Gens d'Armes

Relive history The boulevard du Palais entrance leads into the hauntingly lit Salle des Gens d'Armes. This hall is considered one of the finest examples of secular Gothic architecture in Europe. The curious spiral staircase on the right of the hall once led to the Great Ceremonial Hall on the upper floor of the palace. Off the Salle des Gens d'Armes is the gloomy Salle des Gardes; this acted as an antechamber to the now-vanished Grand'Chambre on the upper floor, where the Revolutionary Tribunal sat in 1793. Across the corridor known as the rue de Paris is the Galerie des Prisonniers, where lawyers, prisoners and visitors mingled. Here are re-creations of the concierge's and clerk's offices, as well as the Salle de Toilette, where prisoners were prepared for execution. At the far end is a poignant re-creation of Marie-Antoinette's cell.

THE BASICS

paris-conciergerie.frr

🔢 J6

✉ 2 boulevard du Palais, Île de la Cité, 75001

☎ 01 53 40 60 80

🕐 Daily 9.30–6 (ticket office 5.30); times may vary

Ⓜ Cité, Châtelet

🚌 21, 24, 27, 38, 58, 70, 81, 85, 96

💶 Moderate (joint ticket with Sainte-Chapelle or Notre Dame expensive)

❓ Guided tours Wed 2.30 and Sat 10.30

4 Galerie Vivienne and the Passages Couverts

OUVERTURE
DU LUNDI AU DIMANCHE

Centered on the 2nd *arrondissement* is a hidden network of interconnecting 19th-century shopping arcades or *passages couverts* that enable you to stroll under cover most of the way from the Palais Royal to the Grands Boulevards and beyond.

Galerie Vivienne Between the late 18th and early 19th centuries the Right Bank included a network of 140 covered passageways—the fashionable shopping malls of the time. Of those that survive, the Galerie Vivienne (1823) is perhaps the most glamorous, squeezed in between the Bibliothèque Nationale and the place des Victoires. You can track down designer clothes—Jean-Paul Gaultier was one of the first to open a shop here—or shop for unusual toys. It's perfect for a rainy day.

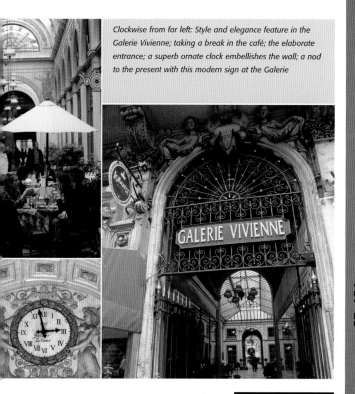

Clockwise from far left: Style and elegance feature in the Galerie Vivienne; taking a break in the café; the elaborate entrance; a superb ornate clock embellishes the wall; a nod to the present with this modern sign at the Galerie

Galerie Colbert Galerie Vivienne's nearby neighbor Galerie Colbert (1826) is as elegant, but lacks shops as it is part of the Institut National de l'Histoire de l'Art. Don't miss the 19th-century brasserie, Le Grand Colbert.

More offbeat browsing These interlinked arcades thread their way north from rue Saint-Marc across the boulevard de Montmartre and into the 9th *arrondissement*. The labyrinthine Passage des Panoramas (1800) is a little tired in places but full of inexpensive restaurants and stamp dealers. Facing it across boulevard de Montmartre is the Passage Jouffroy (1845), where the quirkiest of the boutiques, La Galerie Fayet, sells antique walking canes. Farther north still, the quieter Passage Verdeau (1847) has vintage book dealers.

THE BASICS

galerie-vivienne.com

✚ H4–H3

✉ Galerie Vivienne: 4 rue des Petits-Champs/6 rue Vivienne, 75002

🍴 Passage 53 (▷ 149), Passages des Panoramas: 10 rue Saint-Marc, 75002

🚇 Bourse, Palais-Royal, Grands Boulevards

🚌 20, 29, 39, 48, 67, 74, 85

♿ Good

🎟 Free

HIGHLIGHTS

● The tomb of Napoleon
● Military architecture on a monumental scale
● Suit of armor belonging to King Henry II
● *Napoleon I in the Throne,* painting by Ingres
● The bugle that signaled the armistice at the end of WW1
● Enigma cryptography machine from WWII

TIP

● The museum app provides useful background information to the displays.

Also known as Hôtel national des Invalides, this splendid complex still provides care and shelter for France's military veterans. But it's best known around the world as the resting place of the country's most famous son, Napoleon Bonaparte.

History of the Complex In 1670 King Louis XIV commissioned architect Liberal Bruant to build the hospital to look after wounded soldiers and to provide shelter for homeless veterans. The massive complex, measuring 643ft along it's river frontage, was finished in 1708.

Musée de l'Armée Les Invalides is home to the Army Museum, one of the largest museums devoted to military history in the world. Created in 1905, the collection is divided into several

Clockwise from top left: Majestic Église du Dôme; a fresco by French artist Charles de la Fosse adorns the inside of the church's cupola; Les Invalides by night; tributes to France's military take place in the square facing the Cour d'Honneur (Court of Honor); Napoleon's tomb within Église du Dôme

departments. Lovers of late medieval history will enjoy the section relating to weapons of the 13th to the 17th century, whilst the most modern exhibitions concentrate on 1871 to 1945, the era that shaped contemporary Europe, including the Franco-Prussian War and the two World Wars. There's a gallery here devoted to the wartime leader Charles de Gaulle.

Tomb of Napoleon Napoleon Bonaparte died in exile on the remote island of St Helena in 1821. His ashes were returned to France in 1840 and interred here in 1861, 40 years after his death. The Dôme des Invalides was built as the royal chapel of the Invalides complex. The tomb of red quartzite set atop a green granite base takes center stage in the rotunda. Visitors view the tomb from a marble gallery.

THE BASICS

musee-armee.fr

✚ D6

✉ 129 rue de Grenelle, 75007

☎ 08 10 11 33 99

🕐 Apr–Oct daily 10–6; Nov–Mar 10–5 (Dome until 7pm Jul–Aug. Last admission 30 mins before closing). Museum closed first Mon of month (except Jul–Sep).

🍴 Restaurant/Bar Le carré des Invalides ($)

🚇 La Tour Maubourg, Ecole Militaire, Varenne

🚌 63, 83, 93

♿ Good

❓ Downloadable app, concert season

🎤 Moderate

6 Jardin du Luxembourg

HIGHLIGHTS

- Médicis fountain
- Musée du Luxembourg
- Bandstand
- Statue of Delacroix
- Orangerie
- Experimental orchard
- Beekeeping school
- Statues of queens of France

Despite the crowds, these gardens are serene in all weathers and are the epitome of French landscaping. This idealized image of an unhurried Parisian existence is a world away from the big-city bustle nearby.

Layout Radiating from the large octagonal pond in front of the Palais du Luxembourg (now the Senate) are terraces, paths and a wide tree-lined alley that leads down to the Observatory crossroads. Natural attractions include shady chestnuts, potted orange and palm trees, an orchard and tropical hothouses. Statues of the queens of France and artists and writers are dotted about.

Park activities All year round joggers pound the circumference and in summer sunbathers

Clockwise from far left: Strolling in front of the Palais du Luxembourg; detail of the Médicis fountain; relaxing in the gardens; bronze statue, l'Acteur Grec, by Charles-Arthur Bourgeois; the gardens provide the perfect setting for a game of chess

settle into park chairs or lie on the grass, card- and chess-players claim the shade in front of the Orangerie, bands tune up at the bandstand near the boulevard Saint-Michel entrance and children burn off energy on swings and donkey rides. Fountains, tennis courts, beehives, a puppet theater and children's playgrounds offer other distractions. In the northwest corner of the park is Paris's oldest public museum, the Musée du Luxembourg. Opened in 1750, it became the first contemporary art museum in 1818 and today stages major temporary exhibitions of art.

Inspiration The Palais du Luxembourg and gardens were commissioned by Marie de Médicis, wife of Henri IV, in 1615, and designed to resemble her childhood Florentine home.

THE BASICS

➕ G8/H8
✉ Main entrance place Edmond Rostand, 75006
☎ Park 01 42 34 20 00. Musée du Luxembourg 01 40 13 62 00, museeduluxembourg.fr
🕐 Park daylight hours. Museum daily 10–7.30 (until 10pm Mon and Fri)
🍴 Open-air café, kiosk
Ⓜ Odéon
🚌 21, 38, 58, 82, 84, 85, 87, 89, 93 (to museum)
🚆 RER Line B, Luxembourg
♿ Very good
💲 Park free; museum expensive

7 Jardin des Tuileries

HIGHLIGHTS

● Jeu de Paume
● Orangerie
● Outdoor sculptures
● Views

Forming a verdant link between the Louvre and the Champs Elysées, the Jardin des Tuileries is perhaps Paris's most visited green space. Here history meets contemporary life as office workers eat lunch and families relax amongst the fine formal gardens that started life as a private park for the French royal family.

Good views This is also a place from where visitors can see several of the city's main attractions. There are good views of the Louvre, the Eiffel Tower, the Musée d'Orsay across the river and up to the Arc de Triomphe at the top of the Champs-Élysées.

Design notes The formal design of the gardens can be credited to the landscape

Clockwise from left: The huge Ferris wheel offers wonderful views of Paris; the boating lake is popular with children; a stroll in the gardens is a great way to spend a few hours and see the outdoor art

architect André le Nôtre, who was gardener to King Louis XIV and the man responsible for the spectacular gardens at Versailles. Le Nôtre laid out the Tuileries in 1664, and over 300 years later they are still being enjoyed.

Activities In one corner is a boating pond, and at the opposite end, overlooking the place de la Concorde, are two of the city's finest small galleries, the Orangerie (▷ 71–72) and the Jeu de Paume (▷ 51). The latter gets its name from the fact that it was once a real tennis court (*jeu de paume*) and the former a warm winter home for the orange trees from the Jardin. There is plenty of outdoor art in the gardens, too. Works by Giacometti, Rodin and Henry Moore are on display, along with several bronzes by Aristide Maillol.

THE BASICS

- ✚ F4–5/G4–5
- ✉ 113 rue de Rivoli, 75001
- ⏰ Jun–Aug daily 7am–11pm; Apr–May, Sep 7am–9pm; Oct–Mar 7.30–7.30
- 🍴 Cafés
- Ⓜ Tuileries
- 🚌 24, 42, 48, 68, 72, 73, 84
- ♿ Good
- 🎫 Free

8 Marché aux Puces de Saint-Ouen

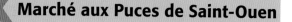

HIGHLIGHTS

● Marché Serpette: art, high-quality furniture
● Marché Paul Bert: trendy items, including classic modern furniture
● Marché Jules Vallès: bric-a-brac
● Marché Biron: antiques, glass, art deco

TIP

● The market area is very extensive, so pick up a free map from the tourist office at 7 impasse Simon by the Marché Paul Bert.

A Sunday pastime popular with many locals is to look for bargains at the city's flea markets, of which the *crème de la crème* is still this one. Nowhere else will you find such a fascinating cross-section of Parisian society.

Duck and banter The approach from the Métro station to this sprawling 7ha (17-acre) market is uninspiring as it entails bypassing jeans and sportswear stalls before ducking under the Périphérique overpass and finally entering the fray. Persevere and you may discover an antique gem, a fake or a second-hand item. If your budget won't stretch to that, you can choose an old postcard of Paris from the thousands on show. Everything and anything is displayed here and all commerce is carried on in the true bantering style of the

Clockwise from far left: Antiques and curiosities at the market; you'll find classic vintage items as well as art deco pieces at Marché Dauphine; pretty antique basin for sale; collector's items include an array of soda siphons; intricate carving is a feature of French furniture

faubourgs. It pays to get "creatively lost," since the most intriguing vendors are not necessarily the ones with the most prominent sites. In particular, don't miss the upper level if you're visiting the Marché Dauphine.

Bargain hard Registered dealers are divided into more than a dozen official markets, which interconnect through busy passageways. Along the fringes are countless hopefuls who set up temporary stands to sell goods ranging from obsolete kitchenware to old jukeboxes and junk. Although unashamedly a tourist trap, there is something for everyone here, but do go early. Bargaining is obligatory. Stop for lunch in one of the bistros along the rue des Rosiers or try the terrace of the café-theater A Picolo at 58 rue Jules-Vallès, which has occasional jazz concerts.

THE BASICS

marcheauxpuces-
saintouen.com
➕ See map ▷ 115
✉ Porte de Clignancourt, 75018
☎ 01 40 11 77 36
🕐 Sat 9–6, Sun 10–6, Mon 10–5 (reduced hours in Aug)
🍴 Cafés and restaurants on rue des Rosiers
🚇 Porte de Clignancourt
🚌 56, 85
♿ Good
❓ Beware of pickpockets

9 Musée de Cluny – Musée national du Moyen-Âge

HIGHLIGHTS

- *La Dame à la Licorne* (The Lady and the Unicorn) tapestries
- Gold altar front
- *Pilier des Nautes*
- Stone heads from Notre-Dame
- Medieval gardens
- Seventh-century votive crown
- Stained glass
- Abbot's Chapel

Take a deep breath outside this museum, surrounded by re-created medieval gardens, and prepare to enter a time warp that conjures up the days of troubadours and courtly love.

Treasures The Gothic turreted Hôtel de Cluny was built at the end of the 15th century by Abbot Jacques d'Amboise and is one of France's finest examples of domestic architecture of this period. The museum it houses, also known as the Musée de Cluny, has 23,000 objects in its collection, most amassed by Alexandre du Sommerard, a 19th-century medievalist. The most famous exhibits are the beautiful *La Dame à la Licorne* tapestries (late 15th century). Costumes, accessories, textiles and tapestries are of Byzantine, Coptic or European

Clockwise from far left: Stone staircase, bathed in lights, in the Gothic Hôtel de Cluny; exterior of the building, now housing the museum; detail of a religious painting displayed in the museum; exterior courtyard, once the site of ancient Roman baths; detail of shells on the exterior

origin, while the gold and metalwork room has outstanding pieces of Gallic, Barbarian, Merovingian and Visigothic artistry. Room VIII houses 21 stone heads knocked from statues on the west front of Notre-Dame. Stained glass, table games, ceramics, wood carvings, illuminated manuscripts and Books of Hours, altarpieces and religious statuary complete this exceptional display.

Baths The late-Roman baths of Lutetia, which comprise cold (frigidarium), tepid (tepidarium) and hot (caldarium) rooms, form part of the museum complex. The most substantial surviving element is the frigidarium, whose restored 14.7m (48ft) vaulted ceiling, makes it one of the most important structures from antiquity to survive north of the Loire.

THE BASICS

musee-moyenage.fr

➕ J7

✉ 6 place Paul-Painlevé, 75005

☎ 01 53 73 78 00

🕐 Wed–Mon 9.15–5.45. Last admission 30 mins before closing.

Ⓜ Cluny–La Sorbonne

🚌 21, 27, 38, 63, 85, 86, 87

Ⓡ RER Line B, Cluny

♿ Moderate; free first Sun of every month

❓ Renovations ongoing. For information on guided tours tel: 01 53 73 78 16

- Palace of Khorsabad
- Glass pyramid entrance, designed by I.M. Pei
- *Bataille de San Romano*, Uccello
- *Mona Lisa*, da Vinci
- Napoleon III apartments
- Vénus de Milo
- Cour Carrée at night
- The Marly Horses

- To avoid the crowds, visit early morning or Wednesday or Friday evening.

Nocturnal lighting transforms the Louvre's glass pyramid entrance into a gigantic cut diamond—just a foretaste of the treasures contained within.

The world's largest museum Originally a medieval fortress, the Louvre first took shape as a private art gallery under François I, eager to display his Italian loot. Henri IV added several galleries, completed in 1610. After escaping the excesses of the Revolutionary mob, it became a people's museum in 1793 and was later enlarged by Napoleon I, who also enriched its collection. Today the Louvre remains a vibrant and exciting art gallery. Its star attraction, the iconic *Mona Lisa,* hangs in its own room which has been specially refurbished to make viewing the painting easier.

Clockwise from far left: All glass and light, the interior of the Louvre; a view across the fountains to the famous glass pyramid; The Raft of the Medusa by Théodore Géricault; detail of the glass pyramid; sculptures in the Richelieu Wing

Art fortress The vast collection of some 35,000 exhibits is arranged on four floors of three wings: Sully (east), Richelieu (north) and Denon (south), while beneath the elegant Cour Carrée lies the keep of the original medieval fortress. Almost 5,000 years of art are covered at the museum, starting with Egyptian antiquities and culminating with European painting up to 1848. Islamic art from three continents is showcased in a contemporary space within the Cour Visconti.

Making the most of your visit There is no way that you'll be able to see everything in one visit, so you'll need to be selective. The free museum map, available from the information desk, highlights the key works and is useful when planning your visit.

THE BASICS

louvre.fr

⊞ H5

✉ 99 rue de Rivoli, 75058. Enter via Pyramid or Carrousel

☎ 01 40 20 53 17; Auditorium 01 40 20 55 55

🕐 Wed–Mon 9–6 (until 9.45pm Wed, Fri)

🍽 Restaurants and cafés

Ⓜ Palais-Royal–Musée du Louvre

🚌 21, 24, 27, 48, 68, 69, 72, 81, 95

♿ Excellent

💰 Expensive; temporary exhibitions expensive; free first Sun of month Oct–Mar

❓ Tours, audio guides, lectures, films, workshops, concerts. Buy your ticket online to save a long wait

★ 11 Musée Marmottan Monet

The Marmottan Monet Museum, in the residential 16th *arrondissement*, houses a mesmerizing collection of Monet paintings, including many colorful canvases of the artist's home in Giverny.

Rich donations This often overlooked treasure of Parisian culture offers an eclectic collection built up over the years from the original donation of Renaissance and First Empire paintings and furniture bequeathed by the art historian Paul Marmottan in 1932. His elegant 19th-century mansion, furnished with Renaissance tapestries and sculptures and Napoleonic furniture, was later given an extra boost by the stunning Wildenstein collection of 313 pages from illustrated manuscripts from the 13th to the 16th centuries, as well as an exceptional

Clockwise from far left: An elegant room used to display Impressionist paintings; visitors admiring the works of Claude Monet and his contemporaries

donation from Michel Monet of works by his father Claude, the Impressionist painter. Other generous donations include works by Monet's contemporaries Gauguin, Renoir, Boudin, Pissarro, Sisley, Berthe Morisot and Gustave Caillebotte, but it is Monet's canvases of dappled irises, wisteria and water lilies, from his last years at Giverny, that are among the most sought out and memorable.

Visiting the museum The museum shop and Salons Impressionnistes are on the ground floor. You will find more Impressionists and the Salle Monet in the basement, while the Wildenstein collection of illuminated manuscripts is housed in a specially designed room. The museum also stages temporary exhibitions on themes related to its collections.

THE BASICS

marmottan.fr

⊞ See map ▷ 114

✉ 2 rue Louis-Boilly, 75016

☎ 01 44 96 50 33

⊙ Tue–Sun 10–6 (Thu until 9). Last admission 30 mins before closing.

Ⓜ La Muette

🚌 22, 32, 52

Ⓡ RER Line C, Boulainvilliers

♿ Moderate

HIGHLIGHTS

● *Olympia*, Edouard Manet
● *Déjeuner sur l'Herbe*, Edouard Manet
● *Les Joueurs de Cartes*, Paul Cézanne
● *La Mère*, James McNeill Whistler
● *L'Angélus*, Jean-François Millet
● *La Cathédrale de Rouen*, Claude Monet
● *Dans un Café*, Edgar Degas
● *La Chambre à Arles*, Vincent van Gogh
● *Femmes de Tahiti*, Paul Gauguin
● Chair by Charles Rennie Mackintosh

TIP

● A Paris Museum Pass (▷ 170) allows you to skip the lines for tickets.

You'll either love or hate the conversion of this 1900 train station. But whatever your view, its art collections, covering the years from 1848 to 1914, are a must for anyone interested in this crucial art period.

Monolithic When this museum finally opened in 1986 controversy ran high: Gae Aulenti's heavy stone structures lay unhappily under Laloux's delicate iron-and-glass shell, built as a train terminus in 1900. But the collections redeem this faux pas, offering a solid overview of the momentous period from Romanticism to Fauvism. Works by the giants of French art—Degas, Monet, Cézanne, Van Gogh, Renoir, Sisley and Pissarro—are the biggest crowd pullers. The opulent restaurant of the old Hôtel d'Orsay on the first floor is a historic monument.

Clockwise from far left: Check out the view through the giant clock in the museum's café; memories of a train station are evoked on the vast ground floor; the ornate station clock; the Musée d'Orsay sits elegantly beside the River Seine

Other highlights You can also see paintings that are examples of Naturalism, Symbolism and the Nabis School. There are sculptures by Rodin, Émile-Antoine Bourdelle and Aristide Maillol, and art nouveau furniture. Save time for the Salle des Fêtes (room 51), tucked away at the end of the middle level. The extravagantly mirrored room with its many chandeliers was originally part of the station's hotel.

Take a tour The chronological tour of the gallery starts with the Impressionists (including Manet, Degas, Monet, Renoir and Sisley) on Level 5, with Post-impressionists (including Van Gogh, Gauguin and Seurat) on the median level below, along with a sculpture gallery. A strong program of temporary exhibitions enhances the permanent collection.

THE BASICS

musee-orsay.fr

+ F5

✉ 62 rue de Lille, 75007

☎ 01 40 49 48 14

🕐 Tue–Sun 9.30–6, Thu 9.30am–9.45pm

🍴 Restaurant on first floor; Café Campana and Café de l'Ours

Ⓜ Solférino

🚌 24, 63, 68, 69, 73, 83, 84, 94

Ⓡ RER Line C, Musée d'Orsay

♿ Excellent

💰 Moderate; free first Sun of the month

❓ Audio and guided tours, concerts and lectures

HIGHLIGHTS

- Ceramics
- *Man with a Guitar*
- Studies for *Les Demoiselles d'Avignon*

TIP

- The museum operates alongside other domestic and international cultural institutions, donating works for temporary exhibitions. As a result, gallery displays will change periodically.

Housing the largest collection of works by Picasso in the world, the Picasso Museum showcases the immense breadth of the artist and, with the art and objects he chose himself, offers an insight into the man.

Taxes After Picasso died in 1973, his family owed about $50 million in death duties. In lieu of this they gave the state 203 of Picasso's paintings, 158 sculptures and many other items including curios he had collected and paintings by other artists. When his widow died in 1986, further works were handed over. The result forms the basis of this remarkable collection covering all periods of the artist's life.

Hôtel Salé The building itself is a delight, originally built in the 1650s by a man who

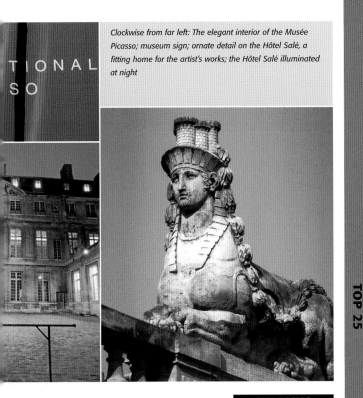

Clockwise from far left: The elegant interior of the Musée Picasso; museum sign; ornate detail on the Hôtel Salé, a fitting home for the artist's works; the Hôtel Salé illuminated at night

gained his own wealth from collecting the very unpopular salt tax that was levied in France at the time. In 1968 it was declared a historic monument, and it opened as the Musée Picasso in 1985. In the last ten years the museum has undergone a $62-million renovation that has greatly enhanced the visitor experience.

The collection Spread over three floors, the collection does not contain the artist's best-known works, such as *Guernica*, but displays many works that he wanted to keep for himself. After all, he once declared himself the greatest collector of Picassos in the world. Works ranging from his Blue Period through to cubism and surrealism showcase the astonishing range of his talents.

THE BASICS

musee-picasso.fr

L5

Hôtel Salé, 5 rue de Thorigny, 75003

01 85 56 00 36

Tue–Fri 10.30–6, Sat–Sun 9.30–6. Last admission 45 mins before closing

Café

Saint-Paul, Saint-Sébastien–Froissart

Very good

Audioguide. Tours in English on Sundays

Expensive; free first Sun of the month

14 Musée du quai Branly – Jacques Chirac

- A glass tower of 9,000 musical instruments
- Nepalese ritual lamp
- Aztec statues
- The Harter bequest of masks and sculptures from Cameroon

TIP

- The museum gardens are particularly magical in the evening, when they are beautifully illuminated.

This eye-catching museum, founded by former French President and Mayor of Paris Jacques Chirac, is dedicated to the cultural heritage of Africa, Asia, Oceania and the Americas.

A 21st-century venue Built on five levels and crowned by a wide terrace with fine views of the Eiffel Tower, the museum is hidden from view by trees and thick vegetation. *Le mur végétal* (plant wall) on the north facade is festooned with 15,000 plants representing 150 species from all over the world.

The collection A swooping white ramp leads through a tunnel to the display area, where you are greeted by a 10th-century anthropomorphic Dogon wood statue from Mali, its one

Clockwise from far left: Plants from all over the world cover the exterior of the museum; head of a figurine from Ifa, Nigeria, dating from the 12th to 14th century; Oceania Gallery; Uli wooden sculpture, 18th to early 19th century, from New Ireland, Oceania

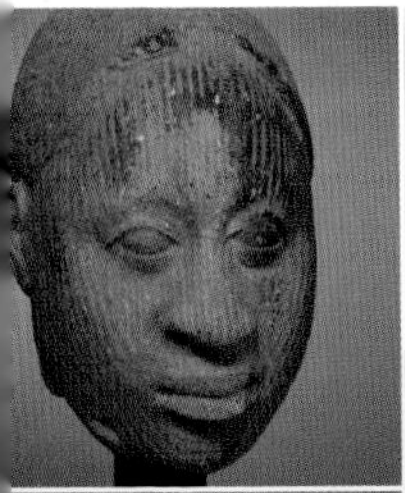

remaining arm reaching skywards. This splendid beginning sets the tone for other highlights, including painted animal hides from the Americas, decorated with battle scenes and abstract earth and sky motifs; a glass tower of 9,000 musical instruments gathered from all corners of the world; and a headdress from Malekula Island, worn by dancers during rituals in the early 20th century. To aid navigation through the museum, each of the different regions has its own floor coloring.

Other attractions The museum stages several temporary exhibitions each year, as well as drama, dance and music in the theater, and hosts debates on historic and contemporary issues. It also has a cinema and holds regular hands-on workshops for adults and children.

THE BASICS

quaibranly.fr

➕ B5

✉ 37 quai Branly, 75007 (also access via 218 rue de l'Université)

☎ 01 56 61 70 00; Ticketline 01 56 61 71 72

🕐 Sun, Tue–Wed 11–7, Thu–Sat 11–9

🍴 Les Ombres (on the roof terrace, tel 01 47 53 68 00) and Café Branly

🚇 Alma–Marceau

🚌 69, 82

🚆 RER Line C, Pont de l'Alma

♿ Good

🎫 Moderate; gardens free

TOP 25

The enchanting Musée Rodin showcases an outstanding collection of the popular artist's work as well as representations of some of his contemporaries.

Hard times Built in 1730, the rococo Hôtel Biron, which houses the Rodin museum, has an interesting history. One owner (the Duc de Lauzun) was sent to the guillotine and the house has been used successively as a dance hall, convent, school and artists' studios. Rodin lived here from 1908 until his death in 1917. In 1919 the house became a museum. The renovated chapel in the grounds is now used for temporary exhibitions.

Sculpture The elegant, luminous interior houses the collection that Rodin left to the

Clockwise from far left: The most famous Rodin sculpture, The Thinker, in the gardens; the facade of the museum; Rodin sculptures around the gardens; detail from The Burghers of Calais sculpture; the former Hôtel Biron, now housing the museum; more sculptures inside

nation. It ranges from his early sketches to the later watercolors and includes many of his most celebrated white marble and bronze sculptures, including *The Kiss* (*Le Baiser*). There are busts of the composer Mahler and writer Victor Hugo, among others, and a series of studies of Balzac. Alongside the Rodins are examples of work by his peers, in particular his tragic mistress and model, Camille Claudel, as well as Eugène Carrière, Edvard Munch, Renoir, Monet and Van Gogh. Rodin's furniture and antiques complete this exceptional collection.

Retreat The museum's private gardens cover 3ha (7.5 acres) and contain several major sculptures, a pond, flowering shrubs and benches for a quiet read. It's worth buying the garden-only ticket just for a respite from city life.

THE BASICS

musee-rodin.fr

➕ E6

✉ 79 rue de Varenne, 75007

☎ 01 44 18 61 10

🕐 Tue, Thu–Sun 10–5.45. Last admission 5.15

🍴 Peaceful garden café

🚇 Varenne, Invalides

🚌 69, 82, 87, 92

🚆 RER line C, Invalides

♿ Wheelchair access

🎟 Moderate; garden inexpensive

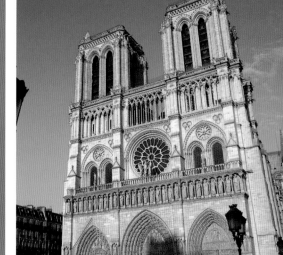

HIGHLIGHTS

- The towers
- Rose windows
- Portals
- Flying buttresses
- The gargoyles
- Emmanuel bell
- Organ
- *Pietà*, Coustou
- Statue of Notre-Dame de Paris (14th-century Virgin and Child)

TIP

- Try to visit just before a service to experience the sense of anticipation as lights are turned on and people gather to worship.

Spectacular is the word to describe this extraordinary monument, with its world-renowned flying buttresses. There are fine views of the cathedral to be had all over the city, including from the river.

Evolution Construction of Notre-Dame started in 1163 and didn't finish until 1345. Since then the cathedral has suffered from pollution, politics, aesthetic trends and religious change. Most of the stained-glass windows were replaced with clear glass (the stained glass was later restored) in the 18th century, when Revolutionary zeal tore down statues and the spire was dismantled. Not least, Viollet-le-Duc, the fervent 19th-century medievalist architect, was let loose on its restoration and initiated radical alterations.

From far left: The awe-inspiring Notre-Dame, which was badly damaged in a fire in 2019; stained-glass windows in the cathedral's Chapelle Saint-Georges; statue of the Virgin and Child

Interior grandeur The hushed, softly lit stone interior contains numerous chapels, tombs and statues. The sacristy on the south side of the choir is where the treasures of Notre-Dame are usually kept. The magnificent stained glass above the mighty organ is one of the largest in Europe. Walk round the outside of the cathedral for a view of its extravagant flying buttresses and iconic towers.

Destruction In April 2019, a fire broke out in a section of the cathedral that was undergoing renovations. The wooden interior was destroyed, which brought down the 93m (305ft) spire and roof, though the stone towers and many of the treasures appear to have been saved. The extent of the damage is still unknown or what this may mean for visitors.

THE BASICS

notredamedeparis.fr
tours-notre-dame-de-paris

➕ J7

✉ Place du Parvis Notre-Dame–Place Jean-Paul II, 75004

☎ 01 42 34 56 10;
Crypt 01 55 42 50 10

🕐 Check online for opening times and advice for visitors following the fire

Ⓜ Cité, Saint-Michel

🚌 21, 38, 47, 58, 70, 85, 96

🚆 RER Lines B and C, Saint-Michel

♿ Good (not in towers)

💰 Cathedral free; towers and Crypt moderate; treasury inexpensive

HIGHLIGHTS

- Grand Staircase
- Grand Foyer
- Auditorium
- Facade
- The shop, Galerie de l'Opéra de Paris (▷ 126)

This ornate wedding cake of a building, with sumptuous details decorating its every surface, presents the perfect epitaph to the frenetic architectural activities of France's Second Empire.

Past glory When Charles Garnier's opera house was inaugurated in 1875 it marked the end of Haussmann's ambitious urban face-lift and announced the cultural transition to the Belle Époque, with Nijinksy and Diaghilev's Ballets Russes as later highlights. The opera house, and a fatal accident with a chandelier in 1896, was the inspiration for the novel *The Phantom of the Opera* (1910) by Gaston Leroux. Today, it stages both dance and opera. Rudolf Nureyev was director of the Paris Ballet here between 1983 and 1989.

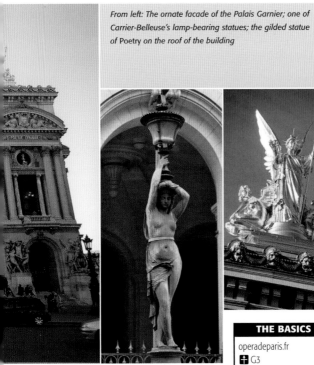

From left: The ornate facade of the Palais Garnier; one of Carrier-Belleuse's lamp-bearing statues; the gilded statue of Poetry on the roof of the building

TOP 25

Dazzle The Palais Garnier's extravagant, regilded facade of arches, winged horses, friezes, columns and much statuary, topped by a verdigris dome, leads into a majestic foyer. This is dominated by the Grand Staircase, dripping with balconies and chandeliers, which sweeps up to the Grand Foyer with its gilded mirrors, marble, murals and Murano glass. Don't miss the equally ornate auditorium, with its dazzling gold-leaf decorations and red-velvet seats, and Marc Chagall's incongruous and, at the time of its installation in 1964, controversial modernist ceiling whose naive scenes pay tribute to great opera and ballet and include recognizable Paris monuments. The auditorium can be visited except during rehearsals. The opera house also has a library and a museum of operatic memorabilia.

THE BASICS

operadeparis.fr

✚ G3

✉ Place de l'Opéra, 75009

☎ 0892 89 90 90 (35¢ per minute)

🕐 Sep to mid-Jul 10–7; late Jul to Aug 10–6; ticket office Mon–Sat 11.30–6.30 (also one hour before performances)

🍴 Restaurant, bar

Ⓜ Opéra

🚌 20, 21, 22, 27, 29, 42, 52, 53, 66, 68, 81, 95

🚇 RER Line A, Auber

♿ Few; tel 01 40 01 18 50

💰 Moderate

❓ Guided tours in English daily 11am and 2.30pm (expensive)

HIGHLIGHTS

- Oscar Wilde's tomb
- Edith Piaf's tomb
- Chopin's tomb
- Marcel Proust's tomb
- Mur des Fédérés
- Delacroix's tomb
- Baron Haussmann's tomb
- Molière's tomb
- Jim Morrison's tomb

TIP

Beware "unofficial" guides loitering by cemetery gates. Book tours through the official website.

If you think cemeteries are somber places then a visit here may change your mind. The plethora of tomb designs, trees and twisting paths create a tranquil setting.

Pilgrimage This landscaped hillside, east of the city center, is a popular haunt for rock fans, Piaf fans and lovers of poetry, literature, music and history. Since its creation in 1804 this vast cemetery has seen hundreds of famous people buried within its precincts, so that a walk around its labyrinthine expanse presents a microcosm of French socio-cultural history. Pick up a map at the entrance or plot your visit in advance on the website.

Tombs and graves The cemetery was created in 1804 on Jesuit land where Louis XIV's

Clockwise from far left: Laid out in 1804 on the slopes of a hill in Ménilmontant, the cemetery is pleasantly shaded by trees; you can find peace and solitude at Père Lachaise; one of the many poignant statues; huge monuments line the wide avenues of the cemetery

TOP 25

confesssor, Father La Chaise, once lived. It was the site of the Communards' tragic last stand in 1871, when the 147 survivors of a night-long fight met their bloody end in front of a government firing squad and were thrown into a communal grave, now commemorated by the Mur des Fédérés in the eastern corner. Memorials also commemorate victims of the Nazi concentration camps. Paths meander past striking funerary monuments and the graves of such well-known people as the star-crossed medieval lovers Abélard and Héloïse, painters Delacroix and Modigliani, actress Sarah Bernhardt, composers Poulenc and Bizet, and writers Balzac and Colette. Crowds of rock fans throng the tomb of Jim Morrison, singer with The Doors, who died in Paris in 1971.

THE BASICS

paris.fr/cimetieres
⊞ See map ▷ 115
✉ Boulevard de Ménilmontant/rue du Repos, 75020
☎ 01 55 25 82 10
🕐 Mid-Mar to early Nov Mon–Fri 8–6, Sat 8.30–6, Sun 9–6; early Nov to mid-Mar Mon–Fri 8–5.30, Sat 8.30–5.30, Sun 9–5.30
🚇 Père Lachaise, Philippe Auguste, Gambetta
🚌 61, 69 ♿ Few
🎫 Free; tours moderate
❓ For information on English-speaking guided tours see Paris Walks (paris-walks.com, tel 01 48 09 21 40)

TOP 25

HIGHLIGHTS

- Jeu de Paume
- Musée de l'Orangerie
  (▷ 71–72)
- Hôtel de Crillon
- *Chevaux de Marly*
  (reproductions)
- View up the
  Champs-Élysées

As you stand in this noisy, traffic-choked square, it is hard to imagine the crowds baying for the deaths of Louis XVI and Marie-Antoinette, who were both guillotined here at the height of the French Revolution.

Gruesome history This pulsating square was initially laid out in the mid-18th century to accommodate a statue of King Louis XV. Under the new name of place de la Révolution, it then witnessed mass executions during the French Revolution and was finally renamed the place de la Concorde in 1795, as revolutionary zeal abated. In the same year, Guillaume Coustou's *Chevaux de Marly* were erected at the base of the Champs-Élysées (today reproductions; the originals are in the Louvre). Crowning the

Clockwise from far left: The ancient Egyptian obelisk takes pride of place; hieroglyphs on the obelisk; detail on a fountain; fountains play in elaborate splendor on the place de la Concorde; statues beneath the fountain; a diagram showing the erection of the obelisk

middle of the Concorde is a 3,000-year-old Egyptian obelisk overlooking eight symbolic statues of French cities. Use the pedestrian crossing to reach the central island for a closer look at the obelisk, framed by two fountains.

Grandeur To the north, on either side of the rue Royale, stand the colonnaded Hôtel de Crillon, one of the finest hotels in the city (on the left), and the matching Hôtel de la Marine (right), home to France's Naval staff, both pre-Revolutionary relics. The rue Royale, with its luxury establishments, leads to the Madeleine. The eastern side of the Concorde is dominated by two public art galleries, both in the Jardin des Tuileries (▷ 26–27). The Jeu de Paume focuses on photography, while nearer the river is the beautifully renovated Orangerie (▷ 71–72).

THE BASICS

🔧 E4–F4

✉ Place de la Concorde, 75008

📷 Jeu de Paume

01 47 03 12 50, jeudepaume.org

🎟 Jeu de Paume Tue 11–9, Wed–Sun 11–7

🚇 Concorde

🚌 24, 42, 72, 73, 84, 94

♿ Jeu de Paume moderate

HIGHLIGHTS

- Pavillon du Roi
- Pavillon de la Reine
- Statue of Louis XIII
- No. 6, Maison de Victor Hugo
- No. 21, residence of Cardinal Richelieu
- Door knockers
- Trompe-l'œil bricks
- Four matching fountains

Paris's oldest and best-preserved square connects the quarters of the Marais and the Bastille. You can marvel at its architectural unity and stroll under the arcades, now animated by outdoor restaurants and window-shoppers.

Place Royale Ever since the square was inaugurated in 1612 with a fireworks display, countless luminaries have chosen to live in the redbrick houses overlooking the central garden of plane trees. Before that, the square was the site of a royal palace, the Hôtel des Tournelles (1388), which was abandoned and demolished by Catherine de Médicis in 1559, when her husband Henri II died there. The arcaded facades were commissioned by Henri IV, who incorporated two royal pavilions at the

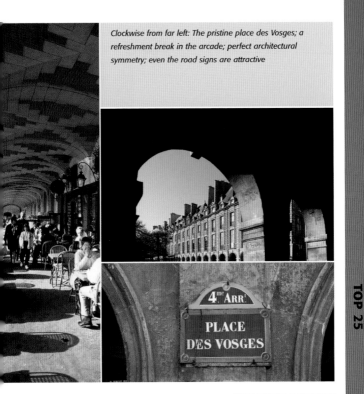

Clockwise from far left: The pristine place des Vosges; a refreshment break in the arcade; perfect architectural symmetry; even the road signs are attractive

heart of the north and south sides of the square and named it place Royale.

Exclusive address After the Revolution the square was renamed place des Vosges in tribute to the first French district to pay its new taxes. The first example of planned development in the city, these 36 town houses, with their steep-pitched roofs, surround a formal garden laid out with gravel paths and fountains, all beautifully symmetrical. The square has attracted many famous residents, including princesses, official mistresses, Cardinal Richelieu, Victor Hugo (his house is now a museum) and Théophile Gautier. Smart shops and chic art galleries, with prices to match, line the square's arcades and are ideal for window-shopping.

THE BASICS

paris.fr
➕ M6
✉ Place des Vosges, 75004
🕐 Maison Victor Hugo Tue–Sun 10–6
🍽 Several
Ⓜ Bastille, Chemin Vert, Saint-Paul
🚌 29, 69, 76
♿ Good
🎫 Free

HIGHLIGHTS

- La Savoyarde bell
- View from the dome
- Mosaic of Christ
- Treasure of Sacré-Cœur
- Bronze doors at Saint-Pierre
- Stained glass
- Statue of Christ
- Statue of the Virgin Mary and Child
- The funicular ride from place Saint-Pierre
- Hearing the choir sing during a service

TIP

- Sacré-Cœur is a pleasant 10-minute walk from Abbesses or Anvers Métro. Or take the Montmartrobus from Abbesses to place du Tertre, from where it's a short walk.

Few people would admit it, but the high point of a trip here is not the basilica itself but the stunning views. You can't forget, however, that Sacré-Cœur was built in memory of the 58,000 dead of the Franco-Prussian War.

Perpetual prayer Although construction started in 1875, it wasn't until 1914 that this white neo-Romanesque-Byzantine edifice was completed, partly due to the problems of laying foundations in the quarry-riddled hill of Montmartre. Priests still work in relays to maintain the tradition of perpetual prayer for forgiveness for the horrors of war and atonement for those slaughtered during the Franco-Prussian war of 1870–71 and, also in 1871, the massacre of some 20,000

Clockwise from far left: Walking up to Sacré-Cœur; equestrian statue of Joan of Arc by Hippolyte Lefèbvre; mosaic of Christ in the basilica; one of the best views in Paris

Communards by government troops. The square bell tower was an afterthought and houses one of the world's heaviest bells, La Savoyarde, which weighs in at 19 tons. The stained-glass windows are replacements of those shattered in WWII.

Panoramas This unmistakable feature of the Paris skyline magnetizes the crowds arriving by funicular or via the steep steps of the terraced garden. For the best views, dawn and dusk offer particularly sparkling panoramas over the city, especially from the exterior terrace of the dome, the second-highest point in Paris after the Eiffel Tower. To the west of Sacré-Cœur is the diminutive Saint-Pierre, a charming church and all that remains of the Benedictine abbey of Montmartre consecrated in 1147.

THE BASICS

sacre-coeur-montmartre.com

✚ c1

✉ Parvis du Sacré-Cœur, 75018

☎ 01 53 41 89 00; Welcome Center 01 53 41 89 09

🕐 Daily 6am–10.30pm; dome and crypt 9.30–8 (5 in winter)

🚇 Abbesses (from here, walk along rue Yvonne Le Tac and rue Tardieu, then take funicular or walk up steps) or Anvers

🚌 Montmartrobus, 30, 31, 54, 67, 80, 85

♿ Wheelchair access from back of basilica

🎟 Basilica free; dome moderate

- Rose window
- Oratory
- Tombs of canons
- Stained-glass depiction of Christ's Passion
- Saint Louis in the "Story of the Relics" window

TIPS

- The upper chapel can become extremely crowded. The quietest times to visit are Tuesday and Friday morning.
- Lines for tickets can be long so buy a ticket at La Conciergerie (▷ 18) if you want to save time.

Sainte-Chapelle's spire, towering 75m (246ft) above the ground, is in itself a great expression of faith, but this is surpassed inside by the glowing intensity of the stained-glass windows climbing to a star-studded roof, now spectacularly restored.

A masterpiece One of Paris's oldest and most significant monuments stands in the precincts of the Palais de Justice. The chapel was built by Louis IX (later canonized) to house the relics he had acquired at exorbitant cost during the crusades, including what was reputed to be the Crown of Thorns, and fragments of the Cross and drops of Christ's blood (now kept in Notre-Dame). Pierre de Montreuil is believed to have masterminded this delicate Gothic construction, bypassing the need for flying

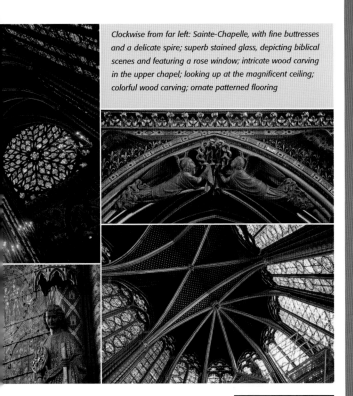

Clockwise from far left: Sainte-Chapelle, with fine buttresses and a delicate spire; superb stained glass, depicting biblical scenes and featuring a rose window; intricate wood carving in the upper chapel; looking up at the magnificent ceiling; colorful wood carving; ornate patterned flooring

buttresses, incorporating a lower chapel for palace servants and installing more than 600 sq m (6,458 sq ft) of striking stained glass above. Completed in 1248 in record time, it was Louis IX's private chapel, with discreet access from what was then the royal palace.

Apocalypse More than 1,000 biblical scenes are illustrated in 15 windows, starting with Genesis to the left of the entrance, and working round the chapel to finish with the Apocalypse, in the rose window. The only non-biblical theme is in the 16th window, which tells how the holy relics came to Paris. Two-thirds of the windows are 13th-century originals—the oldest stained glass in Paris. The statues of the Apostles are copies; the originals are at the Musée de Cluny – Musée national du Moyen-Âge (▷ 30–31).

THE BASICS

sainte-chapelle.fr

➕ J6

✉ 8 boulevard du Palais, Île de la Cité, 75001

☎ 01 53 40 60 80

🕐 Apr–Oct daily 9.30–6 (mid-May to mid-Sep Wed til 9.30pm); Nov–Mar 9–5

Ⓜ Cité, Châtelet

🚌 21, 24, 27, 38, 58, 70 85, 96

🚆 RER Line B, Saint-Michel

♿ Moderate (joint ticket expensive, ▷ panel 56)

❓ Guided tours in English; call for times

THE BOAT TRIP

Distance: 11km (7 miles)
Allow: Just over 1 hour
Start/End: Square du Vert-Galant, Pont Neuf
How to get there:
🚇 Pont Neuf
🚌 24, 27, 58, 67, 70, 72, 74, 75
From the Métro station, walk over the Pont Neuf. About halfway across, on the right, is a sign for the Vedettes du Pont Neuf. Go down the steps to the square.

TIPS

● Evening, when the monuments are lit up, is a great time to go on this trip.
● A more flexible way to enjoy the river is the hop-on, hop-off Batobus shuttle service (▷ 167).

A pleasant river cruise along the Seine is a great way to view some of Paris's key sights from a different perspective. And in just over an hour you can see many of the famous landmarks.

Romantic trip The boat leaves from square du Vert-Galant and heads west. On the Right Bank you can see the Museé du Louvre (▷ 32–33). After passing under the Pont du Carrousel and the Pont Royal you'll see the Musée d'Orsay (▷ 36–37) on the Left Bank and then the 18th-century Palais Bourbon. On the Right Bank is place de la Concorde (▷ 50–51). The boat passes under the ornate Pont Alexandre III (▷ 74). On the Right Bank are the Grand Palais and Petit Palais (▷ 68) and on the Left Bank, in the distance, is Les Invalides (▷ 22–23). After

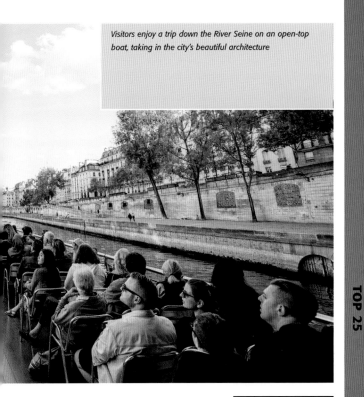

Visitors enjoy a trip down the River Seine on an open-top boat, taking in the city's beautiful architecture

passing under the Pont des Invalides, the Pont de l'Alma and the Passerelle Debilly, the boat rounds a bend to unveil a spectacular view of the Eiffel Tower (▷ 60–61) on the Left Bank. It then passes under the Pont d'Iéna, which spans the river between the Eiffel Tower and the Jardins du Trocadéro, before turning and heading back in the opposite direction to the Île de la Cité. You'll see the cupola of the Institut de France on the right before you pass under the southern side of the Pont Neuf. The next two bridges are the Pont Saint-Michel, leading to the Latin Quarter and the Sorbonne university, and the Petit Pont, the smallest bridge in Paris. On the Île de la Cité you can see Notre-Dame cathedral (▷ 44–45); the boat then circles the picturesque Île Saint-Louis before returning to the Pont Neuf past the Conciergerie.

THE BASICS

vedettesdupontneuf.com
☎ 01 46 33 98 38
🕐 Check online for sailing times
💰 Expensive
❓ Tours in English and French. Pick up a free route map from the boarding platform

HIGHLIGHTS

● Panoramic views
● Gustave Eiffel's office
● Sparkling lights
● Glass floor at level 1

TIPS

● To skip the wait for the elevators, walk up the stairs to level two, then catch the elevator to the top. The climb isn't too daunting. Alternatively, buy your tickets online.
● The wait for the elevator is generally shorter at night.
● Strollers (buggies) are allowed up the tower only if they are collapsible.

The Eiffel Tower could be a cliché but it isn't. The powerful silhouette of Gustave Eiffel's marvel of engineering still makes a stirring sight, especially at night when its delicate, lace-like iron structure is accentuated by lights.

Glittering feat Built in a record two years for the 1889 Exposition Universelle, the Eiffel Tower was never intended to be a permanent feature of the city. However, in 1910 it was finally saved for posterity, preparing the way for today's 6.7 million annual visitors. Avoid a long wait for the elevator by visiting the tower at night, when it fully lives up to its romantic image and provides a glittering spectacle, whether of the illuminated tower itself or of the carpet of nocturnal Paris unfolding at its feet.

Clockwise from far left: The icon of Paris, set in the Champ de Mars; view of the tower from the Jardins du Trocadéro; the tower framed by the Wall of Peace; detail of the lace-like iron structure; the lower section dwarfs the crowds

More than 330 spotlights illuminate the iron latticework, topped by a rotating beacon. After dusk the tower sparkles for 5 minutes every hour on the hour until 1am, thanks to 20,000 randomly flashing low-energy bulbs.

Violent reactions Gustave Eiffel was a master of cast-iron structures. His 324m (1,063ft) tower attracted great opposition, but his genius was vindicated by the fact that it sways no more than 9cm (3.5in) in high winds and remained the world's highest structure for 40 years. Eiffel kept an office here until his death in 1923; at the top, there is a re-creation of Thomas Edison's visit on 10 September 1889. A new 3m-high glass screen now surrounds the base of the tower, increasing sight security yet allowing full view of the city icon.

THE BASICS

toureiffel.paris

➕ B6

✉ Quai Branly, Champ de Mars, 75007

☎ 08 92 70 12 39

🕐 Sep to mid-Jun daily 9.30am–11.45pm; last elevator up at 10.30pm (stairs 9.30–6.30); mid-Jun to Aug 9am–12.45am; last elevator up at 11pm

🍽 Le 58 (1st floor, 08 25 56 66 62); Le Jules Verne (2nd floor, ▷ 149)

Ⓜ Bir-Hakeim, Trocadéro

🚌 42, 69, 82, 87

🚆 RER Line C, Tour Eiffel

♿ Very good (to 2nd floor). Wheelchair users are unable to go to the very top

💰 Expensive; 2nd stage moderate; stairs moderate

HIGHLIGHTS

● Hall of Mirrors
● Petit Trianon
● Formal gardens
● Grandes Eaux
● Hameau and farm
● Buffet d'Eau, Grand Trianon
● Opera house

TIP

● Attend a performance to see the interior of the splendid 18th-century royal opera house.

The Château de Versailles has undergone a massive renovation that has restored much of the grandeur enjoyed by the Sun King, Louis XIV, who commissioned the palace.

A new palace Versailles is the ultimate symbol of French grandeur, and the backdrop to the end of the monarchy in 1789. Louis XIV moved his court to the site of his father's hunting lodge, creating a royal residence, seat of government and home to French nobility. Building continued until his death in 1715, by which time the 100ha (247-acre) garden had been perfected by landscape garden designer André Le Nôtre.

Glorious gardens With their geometric beds, vast watercourses and splendid fountains

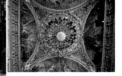

Clockwise from far left: The magnificent château and the elaborate formal gardens; the lawns and lake with the Latona fountain in the foreground; the delightful floral fountain; ceiling detail in the Hall of Mirrors; the stunning Hall of Mirrors, the central feature of the château

THE BASICS

chateauversailles.fr

➕ See map ▷ 114

✉ Place d'Armes, Versailles, 78000

☎ 01 30 83 78 00

🕐 State apartments: Apr–Oct Tue–Sun 9–6.30; Nov–Mar Tue–Sun 9–5.30. Grand and Petit Trianon: Tue–Sun 12–5.30 (until 6.30 in summer). Park: daily 8am–8.30pm (8–6 in winter). Fountains: Apr–Oct Sat–Sun 11–12, 3.30–5 (also late May–late Jun Tue 11–12, 2.30–4)

🚉 RER C, Versailles Rive Gauche

♿ Few (state apartments)

🎫 Passport ticket (1 or 2-day) for all palaces expensive (visitors with disabilities free); park free; Grandes Eaux and Jardins Musicaux moderate Apr–Oct. (If you have tickets, go to the A access. If not, go to Ticket Information, South Ministers' Wing.) Free first Sun of month Nov–Mar

❓ Guided tours

(flowing weekends Apr–Oct), the palace gardens are the perfect expression of the formal French style. Geometry rules, too, in the floral gardens at the lavish royal retreat of Grand Trianon, but Marie-Antoinette's romantic estate at the Petit Trianon is informal and pretty. It comprises a small château, belvedere, a rustic hamlet (Hameau de la Reine) and the notorious but delightful farm where the queen liked to play at being a milkmaid.

Architectural highlights The magnificence of the Hall of Mirrors is the highlight of the Grands Appartements, where you can also access the opulent Queen's Chamber (closed for renovation). At weekends, you can visit the more intimate apartments of the Dauphin and Louis XV's daughters.

More to See

This section contains other great places to visit if you have more time. Some are in the heart of the city while others are a short journey away, found under Farther Afield. This chapter also has fantastic excursions that you should set aside a whole day to visit.

MORE TO SEE

In the Heart of the City

CAFÉ BEAUBOURG

cafebeaubourg.com

Opposite the Pompidou Centre, this café is frequented by artists, critics and book-reading poseurs.

🔠 K5 ✉ 43 rue Saint-Merri, 75004
☎ 01 48 87 63 96 ⏰ Daily 8am–2am. Last orders midnight 🚇 Hôtel de Ville, Châtelet, Rambuteau

CAFÉ LES DEUX MAGOTS

lesdeuxmagots.fr

This famous Left Bank café attracts a mix of tourists and those following in the footsteps of Albert Camus and Ernest Hemingway.

🔠 G6 ✉ 6 place Saint-Germain-des-Prés, 75006 ☎ 01 45 48 55 25 ⏰ Daily 7.30am–1am 🚇 Saint-Germain-des-Prés

CAFÉ DE FLORE

Cafedeflore.fr

Haunted by ghosts of existentialists Sartre and de Beauvoir, who held court here during the German Occupation, this café is pricey but a good spot for people-watching.

🔠 G6 ✉ 172 boulevard Saint-Germain, 75006 ☎ 01 45 48 55 26 ⏰ Daily 7.30am–1.30am 🚇 Saint-Germain-des-Prés

CIMETIÈRE DE MONTMARTRE

Montmartre's cemetery has many graves of the famous, including writers Henri Stendhal and Alexandre Dumas, and artists Edgar Degas and Jean-Baptiste Greuze. The tomb of Émile Zola is near the main entrance, although the writer's remains were moved to the Panthéon in 1908.

🔠 a1 ✉ 20 avenue Rachel, 75018
☎ 01 53 42 36 30 ⏰ Mid-Mar to early Nov Mon–Sat 8–6, Sun 9–6; Nov to mid-Mar Mon–Sat 8–5.30, Sun 9–5.30. Last entry 15 mins before closing 🚇 Place de Clichy, Blanche

DOMAINE NATIONAL DU PALAIS ROYAL

domaine-palais-royal.fr

Elegant 18th-century shopping arcades surround this garden and palace (now the Conseil Constitutionnel and the Ministère de la Culture). Daniel Buren's striking striped columns occupy the Cour d'Honneur.

🔠 H4 ✉ Place du Palais-Royal, 75001
☎ 01 47 03 92 16 ⏰ Daily 8am–10.30pm
🍴 Plenty 🚇 Palais-Royal–Musée du Louvre

Outside Café les Deux Magots

Monument at the Cimetière de Montmartre

ÉGLISE SAINT-ÉTIENNE-DU-MONT

saintetiennedumont.fr
Dating from the 15th century, this church has a combination of Gothic, Renaissance and classical architecture. The unique screen arching over the nave is a highlight.
➕ J8 ✉ Place Sainte-Geneviève, 75005 ☎ 01 43 54 11 79 🕙 Mon 6.30pm–7.30pm, Tue–Fri 8–7.45, Sat 8.45–12, 2–7.45, Sun 8.45–12.15, 2–7.45 (hours can vary during holidays) 🚇 Cardinal Lemoine

ÉGLISE SAINT-EUSTACHE

saint-eustache.org
Renaissance in decoration and detail but Gothic in general design, this church has frequent concerts.
➕ J4–5 ✉ 2 impasse Saint-Eustache, 75001 ☎ 01 42 36 31 05 🕙 Mon–Fri 9.30–7, Sat–Sun 9–7 🚇 Les Halles

ÉGLISE SAINT-GERMAIN-DES-PRÉS

eglise-saintgermaindespres.fr
Paris's oldest church dates from the 11th century and preserves an original tower and choir. There are organ and concert recitals.

➕ G6 ✉ Place Saint-Germain-des-Prés, 75006 ☎ 01 55 42 81 10 🕙 Daily 8–7.45 🚇 Saint-Germain-des-Prés

ÉGLISE SAINT-MERRI

saintmerry.org
This superb example of Flamboyant Gothic, not completed until 1612, has Renaissance stained glass, murals and an impressive organ loft. It also holds concerts.
➕ J5/K5 ✉ 76 rue de la Verrerie, 75004 ☎ 01 42 71 93 93. See accueilmusical.fr for concert information 🚇 Hôtel de Ville

ÉGLISE SAINT-SÉVERIN

saint-severin.com
Built between the 13th and 16th centuries on the site of an 11th-century church, the church features lovely stained glass and palm-tree vaulting.
➕ J7 ✉ 3 rue des Prêtres Saint-Séverin, 75005 ☎ 01 42 34 93 50 🕙 Mon–Sat 11–7.30, Sun 9–8.30 🚇 Saint-Michel, Cluny–La Sorbonne

ÉGLISE SAINT-SULPICE

Work started here in 1646, ending 134 years later with asymmetrical

Église Saint-Eustache

Église Saint-Germain-des-Prés

towers and mixed styles. Note Delacroix's murals in the first chapel on the right and 18th-century wood paneling in the sacristy.

➕ G7 ✉ Place Saint-Sulpice, 75006 ☎ 01 42 34 59 98 🕐 Daily 7.30–7.30 Ⓜ Saint-Sulpice

GRAND MUSÉE DU PARFUM

grandmuseeduparfum.fr

France has been famed for its fragrance industry for many generations, and several of its most renowned *marques* have consulted on a museum dedicated to the art. The contemporary galleries trace the history of perfume production, from antiquity to today's state of the art techniques.

➕ E3 ✉ 73 rue de Faubourg St Honoré, 75008 ☎ 01 42 65 25 44 🕐 Tue–Sun 10.30–7 Ⓜ Franklin D Roosevelt, Meromesnil 💰 Expensive

GRAND PALAIS AND PETIT PALAIS

grandpalais.fr.petitpalais.paris.fr

These two fine buildings were erected for the Universal Exposition of 1900 in the fashionable beaux-arts style. Today they perform an important arts function. The Petit Palais houses a permanent collection as the Musée des Beaux-Arts with pieces from the Classical era to the early 20th century. The Grand Palais lends its immense space to an eclectic program of exhibitions.

➕ D4/E4 ✉ Grand Palais: avenue du General Eisenhower. Petit Palais: avenue Winston Churchill ☎ Grand Palais: 01 44 13 17 17. Petit Palais: 01 53 43 40 00 Ⓜ Champs-Élysées–Clemenceau

ÎLE SAINT-LOUIS

An oasis of calm, the Île Saint-Louis maintains a spirit of its own. Rue Saint-Louis-en-l'Île is lined with art shops and restaurants.

➕ K7 Ⓜ Pont Marie, Sully Morland

INSTITUT DU MONDE ARABE

imarabe.org

The high-tech reinterpretation of traditional Arab fretwork is the hallmark here. The museum has fine metalwork, ceramics, textiles, carpets and calligraphy.

➕ K7 ✉ 1 rue des Fossés Saint-Bernard,

Vaulted ceiling, Gothic arches and stained glass inside Église Saint-Séverin

75005 ☎ 01 40 51 38 38 ⏰ Tue–Fri 10–6, Sat–Sun 10–7 Ⓜ Cardinal Lemoine, Jussieu 🅿 Moderate

MAISON EUROPÉENNE DE LA PHOTOGRAPHIE

mep-fr.org

This is a stylish complex for contemporary photography, with dynamic temporary shows. The galleries are spread over five floors of the 18th-century Hôtel Hénault de Cantobre and a new wing.
➕ L6 ✉ 5–7 rue de Fourcy, 75004 ☎ 01 44 78 75 00 ⏰ Wed–Sun 11am–7.45pm Ⓜ Saint-Paul 🅿 Moderate

MÉMORIAL DE LA SHOAH

memorialdelashoah.org

This moving Holocaust museum contains a wall inscribed with the names of the 76,000 Jewish people deported from France between 1942 and 1944. It also mounts temporary exhibitions on Holocaust-related themes.
➕ K6 ✉ 17 rue Geoffroy-l'Asnier, 75004 ☎ 01 42 77 44 72 ⏰ Sun–Fri 10–6 (Thu until 10) Ⓜ Saint-Paul, Hôtel de Ville, Pont Marie 🅿 Free

MUSÉE D'ART ET D'HISTOIRE DU JUDAÏSME

mahj.org

Jewish art and culture are on display here, from medieval times to the present day, in France but also the rest of Europe and North Africa. Exhibits range from wedding items, *objets d'art*, detailed manuscripts and textiles to the work of Jewish artists such as Modigliani and Chagall.
➕ K5 ✉ Hôtel de Saint-Aignan, 71 rue du Temple, 75003 ☎ 01 53 01 86 60 ⏰ Mon–Fri 11–6, Sat–Sun 10–6. Last admission 45 mins before closing Ⓜ Rambuteau, Hôtel de Ville 🅿 Moderate

MUSÉE D'ART MODERNE DE LA VILLE DE PARIS

mam.paris.fr

The collection here covers fauvism, cubism, surrealism, abstract and Nouveau Réalisme. The museum occupies the east wing of the Palais de Tokyo; the west wing houses the Centre d'Art Contemporain. Note: The museum is undergoing renovations until 2019, but will remain open during this period.

A sign at the Maison Européenne de la Photographie

Musée d'Art et d'Histoire du Judaïsme

➕ B4 ✉ 11 avenue du Président Wilson, 75016 ☎ 01 53 67 40 00 🕐 Tue–Wed, Fri–Sun 10–6, Thu 10–10. Last admission 45 mins before closing 🚇 Iéna, Alma–Marceau 💲 Free; temporary exhibitions moderate

MUSÉE DES ARTS DÉCORATIFS

lesartsdecoratifs.fr

This collection of decorative arts is enriched by contributions from 20th-century designers such as Le Corbusier, Mallet-Stevens, Niki de Saint Phalle and Philippe Starck. Another branch of the museum is the Musée Nissim Camondo on rue de Monceau, an early 20th-century mansion complete with original decor.

➕ G5 ✉ 107 rue de Rivoli, 75001 ☎ 01 44 55 57 50 🕐 Tue–Sun 11–6 (Thu until 9). Last admission 30 mins before closing 🚇 Palais-Royal–Musée du Louvre 💲 Moderate; combined ticket for all sites expensive

MUSÉE DES ARTS ET MÉTIERS

arts-et-metiers.net

Art meets science at this museum through antique clocks, optics, underwater items including a diving suit, vintage cars and mechanical toys.

➕ K4 ✉ 60 rue Réaumur, 75003 ☎ 01 53 01 82 00 🕐 Tue–Sun 10–6 (Thu until 9.30pm) 🚇 Arts et Métiers, Réaumur–Sébastopol 💲 Moderate

MUSÉE CARNAVALET

carnavalet.paris.fr

This major museum, dedicated to the long history of Paris, is currently closed for renovation work. The work is scheduled for completion in early 2020.

➕ L6 ✉ 23 rue Sévigné, 75003 ☎ 01 44 59 58 58 🚇 Saint-Paul 🚌 29, 69, 76, 96

MUSÉE COGNACQ-JAY

museecogancqjay.paris.fr

In a magnificent Marais mansion furnished in 18th-century style, you can see the 18th-century paintings and *objets d'art* collected by Ernest Cognacq and his wife Louise Jay, founders of the La Samaritaine department store.

➕ L6 ✉ Hôtel Donon, 8 rue Elzévir, 75003 ☎ 01 40 27 07 21 🕐 Tue–Sun 10–6 🚇 Saint-Paul 💲 Free

Musée d'Art Moderne de la Ville de Paris

Modern design at the Musée des Arts Décoratifs

MUSÉE GUSTAVE MOREAU

musee-moreau.fr

This studio-museum, on the edge of Pigalle, presents an intriguing view of how a late-19th-century artist lived and worked. On the second and third floors are the studios of the symbolist painter Gustave Moreau (1826–98), teacher to Henri Matisse; on the first floor is a reconstruction of Moreau's private apartment.

🔲 G2 ✉ 14 rue de la Rochefoucauld, 75009 ☎ 01 48 74 38 50 🕐 Mon, Wed, Thu 10–12.45, 2–5.15, Fri–Sun 10–5.15 🚇 Trinité 💵 Moderate; free first Sun of the month

MUSÉE JACQUEMART-ANDRÉ

musee-jacquemart-andre.com

This elegant mansion was built between 1869 and 1876 for the Parisian financier Eduard André and his wife, the artist Nélie Jacquemart. It is filled with original furniture and a fine collection of paintings, including works by Botticelli, Rembrandt, Bellini, Van Dyck, Fragonard and Jacques-Louis David.

🔲 D2 ✉ 158 boulevard Haussmann,

75008 ☎ 01 45 62 11 59 🕐 Daily 10–6 🚇 Saint-Philippe-du-Roule, Miromesnil 💵 Expensive (audio guide included)

MUSÉE DE MONTMARTRE

museedemontmartre.fr

Montmartre's history includes a headless saint, windmills and a notoriously liberal nightlife. Find out more at the Musée de Montmartre, where you'll find artworks by Toulouse-Lautrec and Modigliani, and the studio of mother and son artists Suzanne Valadon and Maurice Utrillo.

🔲 c1 ✉ 12 rue Cortot, 75018 ☎ 01 49 25 89 39 🕐 Apr–Sep daily 10–7; Oct–Mar 10–6 🚇 Lamarck Caulaincourt, Anvers 💵 Moderate

MUSÉE DE L'ORANGERIE

musee-orangerie.fr

A major repository of 20th-century art, the Orangerie is most famous for Claude Monet's *Water Lilies*, a cycle of paintings donated by the artist in the wake of the WW1 Armistice in 1918. Almost 100 meters in length, this breathtaking eight-canvas wonder is one of

Paintings at the Musée Gustave Moreau

the pivotal works of the Impressionist movement.

⊞ F4 ✉ Jardin des Tuileries, Place de la Concorde, 7500 ☎ 01 44 77 80 07 🕐 Wed–Mon 9–6. Last admission 5.15pm Ⓜ Concorde, Tuileries ✋ Moderate

MUSÉE YVES SAINT LAURENT

museeyslparis.com

Opened in 2017, this museum is housed in the building where Frenchman Yves Saint Laurent (1936–2008) created his haute-couture collections between 1974 and 2002. A constantly changing display showcases his work, from the original sketches that captured his ideas through to the finished catwalk gowns.

⊞ B4 ✉ 5 avenue Marceau, 75116 ☎ 01 44 31 64 00 🕐 Tue–Sun 11–6 (Fri til 9pm). Last entry 45 minutes before closing Ⓜ Alma, Marceau ✋ Moderate

MUSÉUM NATIONAL D'HISTOIRE NATURELLE, JARDIN DES PLANTES

mnhn.fr

Set up in 1635 on the initiative of Louis XIII's physician, the Jardin des Plantes is Paris's botanical garden, complete with an alpine section and hothouses. Around its fringes are the buildings of the Muséum National d'Histoire Naturelle, of which the garden forms part. These include the Galeries de Paléontologie et d'Anatomie Comparée, housing dinosaur skeletons, and the Grande Galerie de l'Évolution which has a children's gallery devoted to biodiversity.

⊞ K9/L9 ✉ 2 rue Buffon, 75005 ☎ 01 40 79 54 79 🕐 Apr–Sep Mon, Wed, Sat–Sun 9–6; Oct–Mar Wed–Mon 9–5 Ⓜ Gare d'Austerlitz, Jussieu ✋ Jardin free, others moderate

PALAIS DE CHAILLOT

Built for the Paris exhibition of 1937, the curving wings of the Palais de Chaillot house the Musée national de la Marine (closed for renovation until 2021), the Musée de l'Homme, the Cité de l'Architecture et du Patrimoine and the Théatre de Chaillot. The wonderfully wide terraced Parvis des Libertés et des Droits de

Aerial view of the Champ de Mars from the Eiffel Tower

l'Homme offers fabulous views across the buildings of Paris.

🔲 A5 ✉ Place du Trocadéro, 75116 ☎ Homme 01 44 05 72 72, museedelhomme.fr; Marine 01 53 65 69 69, musee-marine.fr 🚇 Trocadéro 🎟 Moderate

PANTHÉON

paris-pantheon.fr

Occupying a hilltop site close to the Sorbonne and the Quartier Latin, Jacques-Germain Soufflot's neoclassical 18th-century structure provides an imposing setting for the tombs of France's greatest citizens, including Voltaire, Dumas, Rousseau and Marie Curie. From April to October, you can ascend the dome as part of a guided tour.

🔲 J8 ✉ Place du Panthéon, 75005 ☎ 01 44 32 18 00 🕐 Apr–Sep daily 10–6.30; Oct–Mar 10–6 🚇 Cardinal Lemoine, Maubert–Mutualité 🎟 Moderate

PARC DU CHAMP DE MARS

The lawns of the Champ de Mars stretch out in a rectangular design between the Eiffel Tower and the 18th-century École Militaire.

The Romans fought the Celtic Parisii tribe here in 52BC—the park's name, Field of Mars, refers to the Roman god of war. It wasn't until 1765 that the site became a parade ground for the École Militaire. The park has hosted national celebrations, parades, international exhibitions and horse races. Today it is popular with all.

🔲 B6–C6 ✉ Champ de Mars, 75007 🚇 École Militaire

PAVILLON DE L'ARSENAL

pavillon-arsenal.com

This strikingly designed building houses well-conceived exhibitions on urban Paris past and present, alongside a display on the city's architectural evolution.

🔲 L7 ✉ 21 boulevard Morland, 75004 ☎ 01 42 76 33 97 🕐 Tue–Sun 11–7 🚇 Sully Morland 🎟 Free

PLACE DES ABBESSES

Place des Abbesses is less touristy than place du Tertre, farther up the Montmartre hill, so it's a quieter coffee stop. The magnificent art nouveau Métro entrance here

Art nouveau entrance to the Abbesses Métro station, designed by Hector Guimard

Bronze figures on the Pont Alexandre III

leads into Paris's deepest station, 30m (98.5ft) below ground. It was designed by Hector Guimard (1867–1942) and is one of only three original Guimard entrances left in Paris.

🚇 b2 ✉ Place des Abbesses, Montmartre, 75018 🚇 Abbesses

PONT ALEXANDRE III

Four gilded bronze Pegasus figures watch over this wildly ornate bridge, which forms a link between Les Invalides (▷ 22–23) on the Left Bank and the Grand Palais and Petit Palais (▷ 68) on the Right. Symbolic of the optimism of the Belle Époque, it was built for the 1900 Exposition Universelle.

🚇 D4 ✉ Cours de la Reine/quai d'Orsay 🚇 Invalides, Champs-Élysées–Clémencea

PONT DE L'ALMA

The first Pont de l'Alma was built in 1856 to commemorate a victory over the Russians by the Franco-British alliance in the Crimean War. The bridge was replaced in 1974. The underpass on the Right Bank is where the fatal car crash involving Diana, Princess of Wales, occurred in August 1997. The Liberty Flame near the entrance, a symbol of American and French friendship, has become an unofficial memorial.

🚇 C4–5 ✉ Place de l'Alma/place de la Résistance 🚇 Alma–Marceau

PONT DES ARTS

The pedestrian bridge of 1804 was replaced in 1984 by an iron structure of seven arches crossed by wooden planks. From the center of the bridge there are excellent views of the Seine. This is a popular spot for lovers to stroll.

🚇 H5–6 🚇 Louvre–Rivoli

PONT NEUF

Dating from 1604, Paris's oldest bridge ironically bears the name of New Bridge. The houseless design was highly controversial at the time.

🚇 H6 🚇 Pont Neuf, Île de la Cité

RUE DU CHERCHE-MIDI

César's sculpture on the rue de Sèvres crossroads marks out this typical Left Bank street, home to

Early 17th-century Pont Neuf features 12 stone arches

the famous Poîlane bakery (No. 8) and the Musée Hébert (No. 85).

➕ G7 🚇 Saint-Sulpice

RUE JACOB

Antiques and interior decoration shops monopolize this picturesque stretch. You can detour to the nearby Musée National Eugène Delacroix on rue de Furstenberg.

➕ G6 🚇 Saint-Germain-des-Prés

RUE DES ROSIERS

At the heart of Paris's lively Jewish quarter, this effervescent street is packed with synagogues, kosher butchers and restaurants, and Hebrew bookshops as well as an array of designer boutiques.

➕ L6 🚇 Saint-Paul

RUE VIEILLE-DU-TEMPLE

The pulse of the hip Marais district, this street is dense with bars, cafés, restaurants and boutiques.

➕ K6–L5 🚇 Saint-Paul

SQUARE DU VERT-GALANT

Enjoy a quintessential view of the picturesque bridges and the iconic Louvre in this tiny, pretty park, which is also the perfect place for a picnic.

➕ H6 ✉ Place du Pont-Neuf, 75001 🚇 Pont Neuf

TOUR MONTPARNASSE

tourmontparnasse56.com

When it was constructed in 1973, with its reinforced concrete core, the Tour Montparnasse's 59 floors of smoked glass provoked some indignation. Since then it has become a popular landmark, visible from all over Paris and, from within, its viewing gallery and terrace offer far-reaching views of the city. In mid-2017, plans for a radical redevelopment of the tower were announced. Architects Nouvel AOM will create a "green" facade with terraced gardens which will soften the once controversial and now dated box-like original shape. Tour Montparnasse will reopen to coincide with the summer 2024 Paris Olympics.

➕ F9 ✉ 33 avenue du Maine, 75015 🚇 Montparnasse–Bienvenüe

Buildings reflected in a Lanvin shop window at rue du Faubourg Saint-Honoré

Square du Vert-Galant

Farther Afield

FONDATION LOUIS VUITTON

fondationlouisvuitton.fr

Designed by architect Frank Gehry, this superb futuristic edifice houses a museum that showcases the art collections of the world-famous Louis Vuitton French haute-couture house.

🔄 See map ▷ 114 ✉ 8 avenue du Mahatma Gandhi, Bois de Boulogne, 75116 ☎ 01 40 69 96 00 🕐 Mon, Wed, Thu 11–8, Fri 11–11, Sat–Sun 9–9 (closed Tue); during French school holidays Sat–Thu (including Tue) 9–9, Fri 9am–11pm 🚇 Les Sablons; minibus from place Charles de Gaulle every 15 mins (ticket €2) 💰 Moderate

LA GRANDE ARCHE

lagrandearche.fr

This modernist echo of the Arc de Triomphe in white marble and on a grand scale was designed by Johann Otto von Spreckelsen. It's a prominent landmark on the city skyline.

🔄 See map ▷ 114 ✉ 1 parvis de La Défense, 92044 ☎ 01 40 90 52 20 🕐 Daily 10–7 🚇 Grande Arche de La Défense 💰 Moderate

La Grande Arche in La Défense

PARC ANDRÉ-CITROËN

Divided into specialist gardens, this 1990s park lies on the site of a former Citroën factory. You'll find zany experimentation with metal and water, plus a tethered balloon.

🔄 See map ▷ 114 ✉ Rue Cauchy, 75015 🕐 Summer daily 8–dusk (9–dusk rest of year) 🚇 Balard, Javel 💰 Free

PARC DES BUTTES CHAUMONT

The loveliest of Haussmann's parks owes its singular beauty and fine views to its craggy site, a former quarry in the northeast of the city. There is also a children's puppet theater, the Guignol de Paris.

🔄 See map ▷ 115 ✉ 1 rue Botzaris, 75019 🕐 May to mid-Sep daily 7am–10pm; mid-Sep 7am–9pm; Oct–Apr 7am–8pm 🚇 Buttes Chaumont 💰 Free

PARC DE LA VILLETTE

lavillette.com

The Parc de la Villette catapults you into a futuristic world. It offers cultural attractions and leisure activities including a science museum, music complex, hemispheric cinema, exhibition venue and the city's flag-ship concert hall, the Philharmonie de Paris, designed by Jean Nouvel. A covered walkway links the Cité des Sciences et de l'Industrie and the Cité de la Musique–Philharmonie de Paris.

🔄 See map ▷ 115 ✉ Park: 211 avenue Jean-Jaurès, 75019 ☎ Park: 01 40 03 75 75. Cité de Sciences et de l'Industrie: 01 40 04 80 00. Cité de la Musique–Philharmonie de Paris: 01 44 84 44 84 🕐 Cité des Sciences et de l'Industrie: Tue–Sat 10–6, Sun 10–7. Cité de la Musique: Tue–Sat 12–6, Sun 10–6 🍴 Cafés, restaurants 🚇 Park: Porte de Pantin. Cité des Sciences et de l'Industrie: Porte de la Villette 💰 Park: free; Cité des Sciences et de l'Industrie: expensive ❓ Reserve activities as soon as you arrive

Excursions

CHANTILLY

domainedechantilly.com

Picturesque Château de Chantilly is surrounded by attractive parkland, with the forest of Chantilly beyond, and contains a magnificent art collection. One of Europe's leading training venues for racehorses, the town of Chantilly is home to a world-famous racecourse and the Musée du Cheval, housed within the Grandes Écuries—a superb 18th-century stable block.

For five centuries, the domain of Chantilly passed from one branch of the same family to another without ever being sold, starting with the Orgemont family in the 14th and 15th centuries before passing to the Montmorency dynasty, one of France's most powerful families. Chantilly passed in turn to the Bourbon Condés, cousins of the kings of France.

The old château was ruined during the Revolution, but in the late 19th century a splendid reconstruction was commissioned by Henri d'Orléans, Duc d'Aumale, the son of King Louis Philippe, who needed somewhere to house his art collection. This still hangs in the Galerie des Peintures in the manner stipulated by him when he bequeathed Chantilly to the nation. The collection includes works by Raphael and Botticelli, Watteau, Delacroix and Ingrès. The château opened as a museum in 1898, a year after the duke's death. The Grands Appartements are in the Renaissance wing of the Petit Château, adjacent to the main building, and include the charming Grande Singerie, an 18th-century boudoir decorated with images of monkeys and chinoiserie. The fine gardens are the work of several masters, including the oldest areas which were designed by Frenchman André Le Notre.

Distance: 48km (30 miles)

Journey Time: 24 mins (SNCF train)/ 45 mins (RER train)

✉ Chantilly 60500 ☎ 03 44 27 31 80

🕐 Château: Apr–Oct daily 10–6; Nov–Mar 10.30–5. Closed early–late Jan. Grand Stables and Musée du Cheval: same as Château

🚉 Chantilly-Gouvieux SNCF, RER line D; free bus from station to château 💶 Expensive

The delightful Château de Chantilly

A winged statue in the Temple of Love, in the grounds of the Château de Chantilly

DISNEYLAND® PARIS

disneylandparis.com

Disneyland® Paris attracts millions of visitors from countries all around Europe and beyond to its two Parks—Disneyland® Park and Walt Disney Studios® Park. The resort, in the Marne-la-Vallée countryside east of Paris, opened in 1992. The Walt Disney Studios® Park was added in 2002. Other attractions include the Disney Village entertainment complex, seven hotels and even a golf course.

Disneyland® Paris offers the traditional Disney experience with family-friendly attractions such as Main Street USA, with its recreation of small town America in the early 20th century, featuring a steam train and horse-drawn streetcars. There are rides to suit all ages and levels of bravery, from the charming musical journey of "it's a small world" to the lavish Indiana Jones™ and the Temple of Peril ride and Buzz Lightyear Laser Blast—a laser shoot-out. Other white-knuckle rides include Star Wars Hyperspace Mountain and

Sleeping Beauty's Castle

Big Thunder Mountain, a journey on a runaway mine train. Minimum height and age restrictions apply on some rides. Every evening (weather permitting), there's a spectacular live show with Disney characters old and new, and the sky is lit up with fireworks and laser lights, all set against the backdrop of the iconic and dreamlike Sleeping Beauty Castle.

Walt Disney Studios® Park's scarier rides include the terrifying Twilight Zone Tower of Terror™—an abandoned art deco hotel in which the elevator plummets faster than the speed of gravity—and the Rock 'n' Roller Coaster starring Aerosmith, a fast, looping roller coaster that accelerates from 0 to 100kph (62mph) in just three seconds.

Much of what there is to see in Walt Disney Studios® Park is movie-related and includes Paris's very own Gallic Disney attraction Ratatouille: A Recipe for Adventure, a 4-D experience where you can join talented gastronome Remy the Rat and his sidekick Linguini as they try to outwit Chef Skinner in Gasteau's restaurant. The movie theme continues with the extraordinary Moteurs...Action! Stunt Show Spectacular and an amazing exploration of the history of special effects at Armageddon: les Effets Spéciaux. Toon Studio is all about animation. At Art of Disney Animation®, you'll learn the techniques used to animate a Disney cartoon before getting the opportunity to try it for yourself.

Distance: 44km (27 miles)

Journey Time: 35 mins

✉ Marne-la-Vallée, 77777, Cedex 4
☎ 0825 300 500 🚇 RER Line A, Marne-la-Vallée 💲 Expensive

FONTAINEBLEAU

musee-chateau-fontainebleau.fr

Fontainebleau has witnessed momentous events, including the birth of Louis XIII in 1601 and Napoleon signing his deed of abdication in 1814. Kings went hunting in the forest here as far back as the 12th century.

With more than 1,500 rooms and 53ha (130 acres) of parkland, the royal château of Fontainebleau is, despite its associations with *la chasse*, no mere hunting lodge: It was the only royal and imperial residence in France to be inhabited continuously for seven centuries, and is consequently a showcase for French architecture in the grand style. The surviving medieval keep forms the core of the building, which was extended in splendid Renaissance style under François I and later, in the 17th century, during the reign of Henri IV. A further wing was built during the time of Louis XV; after the Revolution, the château was restored by Napoleon Bonaparte. Its final royal inhabitant was Napoleon III, whose court stayed here until 1869.

The most spectacular of the interiors are the Renaissance rooms, inspired by the new artistic styles François I had seen whilst he was in Italy. These rooms include the sumptuous ballroom and François I's magnificent long gallery. Altogether more intimate in scale are Marie Antoinette's boudoirs and the apartment of Louis XIV's secret second wife, Madame de Maintenon. Outside, the beautiful Grand Parterre is reputedly the largest formal garden in Europe.

Distance: 68km (42 miles)
Journey Time: 50 mins
☎ 01 60 71 50 70 ⓒ Château: Apr–Sep Wed–Mon 9.30–6; Oct–Mar Wed–Mon 9.30–5. Last admission 45 mins before closing. Courtyard and gardens: May–Sep daily 9–7; Mar–Apr, Oct 9–6; Nov–Feb 9–5. Park: daily 24 hours ⓔ Fontainebleau–Avon ⓔ PARISCityVISION runs day tours by coach, departing from rue des Pyramides, 75001 (tel 01 44 55 60 00, pariscityvision. com) ⓦ Château (limited areas only) moderate; courtyard, gardens and park free

Renaissance-style splendor at Fontainebleau

City Tours

This section contains self-guided tours that will help you explore the sights in each of the city's regions. Each tour is designed to take a day, with a map pinpointing the recommended places along the way. There is a quick reference guide at the end of each tour, listing everything you need in that region, so you know exactly what's close by.

CITY TOURS

Around the Tour Eiffel

Long vistas and grandiose public buildings characterize this part of Paris—but at its heart the Eiffel Tower is 324m (1,063ft) of pure, unmissable fun.

Morning

Start in front of the **Musée d'Orsay** (▷ 36–37), but save the museum itself for another day. The Musée National de la Légion d'Honneur across the street sets the tone for a walk that's rich in political and military landmarks. Continue along the quai Anatole France to the Assemblée Nationale, France's lower house of parliament, its dignified neoclassical portico facing the **place de la Concorde** (▷ 50–51) across the river. Continue along quai d'Orsay past the mansion-like ministry of foreign affairs, popularly known by its address and one of the most important architectural monuments of the Second Empire. Until 1973 it was also a residence for high officials; King Juan Carlos of Spain was the last to stay there. Admire the florid, gilded statuary of the **Pont Alexandre III** (▷ 74) before turning left down broad, stately avenue du Maréchal Galliéni, named for a World War I military commander. Ahead of you is the wide, imposing facade of **Les Invalides** (▷ 22–23) which was built by Louis XIV and is the last resting place of Napoleon Bonaparte.

Late morning

Take time to explore the **Musée de l'Armée** (▷ 22), which occupies much of the majestic Les Invalides, before visiting France's national military pantheon, the **Église du Dôme** (▷ 22–23), in which Napoleon's tomb takes pride of place.

Lunch

There's a simple but strategically located café on the south side of the Musée de l'Armée, but for a more substantial lunch in elegant surroundings make a short detour to the **Brasserie Thoumieux** (▷ 146) in rue Saint-Dominique.

Afternoon

Stroll the short distance along avenue de Tourville to reach the enormous École Militaire, constructed during the time of Louis XV and today, still occupied by the military. It faces the **Parc du Champ de Mars** (▷ 73), a vast green space stretching northwest toward the Eiffel Tower. To reach the park, cross the broad cobbled avenue de la Motte-Picquet with care. Amble the length of the Champs de Mars to reach the **Eiffel Tower** (▷ 60–61); buy your tickets in advance online to save time.

Late afternoon

No visit to the Eiffel Tower is complete without crossing the river to experience the classic view of the tower itself. Cross the Pont d'Iéna to reach the **Palais de Chaillot** (▷ 72); save its museums for another day, but go up to the piazza between the two curved wings of the complex for the best view.

Evening

Stick around until after dusk to experience the beauty of the tower's soft golden lighting—and the spectacle of 20,000 flashing lights that make it glitter for five minutes every hour on the hour.

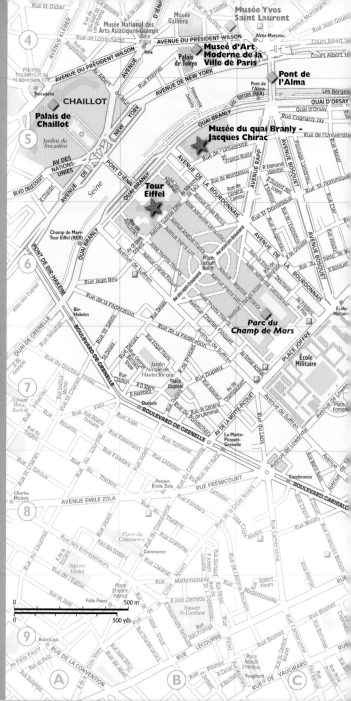

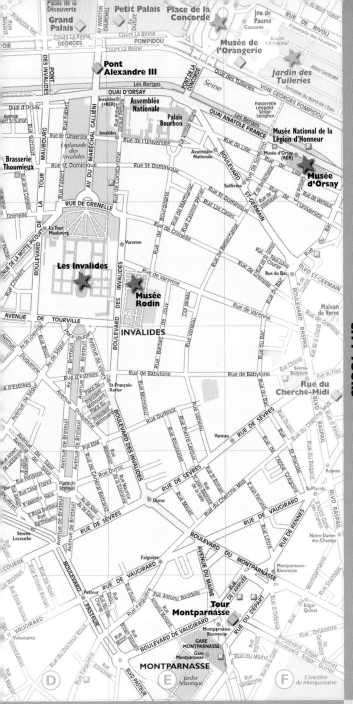

Around the Tour Eiffel
Quick Reference Guide

Les Invalides (▷ 22)
Commissioned by Louis XIV as a military hospital and welfare center, this magnificent complex houses the Army Museum and the tomb of Napoleon Bonaparte.

Musée d'Orsay (▷ 36)
The architectural merit of this audacious conversion of a former railroad station still divides opinion, but its breathtaking collection makes it one of Paris's must-see attractions.

Musée du quai Branly – Jacques Chirac (▷ 40)
The national collection of art from Africa, Asia, Oceania and the Americas is housed in a modernist building by architect Jean Nouvel.

Musée Rodin (▷ 42)
An 18th-century mansion and its peaceful garden are the setting for the sculptures left to the nation by Rodin, along with other works by him and his contemporaries.

Tour Eiffel (▷ 60)
Though it was originally built as a temporary structure for the 1889 Exposition Universelle, it's hard to imagine Paris now without Gustave Eiffel's instantly recognizable tower.

CITY TOURS

Palais de Tokyo courtyard at Musée d'Art Moderne de la Ville de Paris

Latin Quarter, St-Germain and Islands

The area's literary and philosophical associations lend intellectual luster to this tour of the Left Bank; fashion and fine dining bring Parisian élan to the mix; and the loveliness of the Seine and its islands adds a final dash of romance.

Morning

Start at rue Mouffetard, where the food and wine shops ensure a bustling atmosphere from morning onward. Make your way to the church of **Saint Étienne-du-Mont** (▷ 67), worth a quick peek for its flamboyant late Gothic choir, before visiting the **Panthéon** (▷ 73), whose neoclassical dome dominates the Latin Quarter—Paris's university district. A stroll down rue Soufflot brings you to the main entrance of the **Jardin du Luxembourg** (▷ 24–25). At this leafy city park, do as the locals do and read in the sun.

Mid-morning

Leave the park by the exit on busy rue de Vaugirard, then follow the gently curving rue Servandoni and rue Palatine to reach **Église Saint-Sulpice** (▷ 67), another Left Bank church well worth a look—this time for its vast, cathedral-like internal dimensions. From here to the boulevard St-Germain the streets are full of intriguing boutiques; indulge in a spot of window-shopping at the stores of talented French designers such as **Sonia Rykiel** (▷ 129), then polish your intellectual credentials with a leisurely drink on the terrace of **Café Les Deux Magots** (▷ 66) or **Café de Flore** (▷ 66)—these famous cafés were once the haunts of Jean-Paul Sartre and Simone de Beauvoir.

Late morning

The church of **Saint-Germain-des-Prés** (▷ 67) gives its name to one of Paris's most atmospheric quarters, wedged between boulevard St-Germain and the river. The streets are lined with handsome old houses and dotted with small art galleries and antiques shops; tucked into rue de Furstenberg is the Musée National Eugène Delacroix.

Lunch

This is an excellent part of town in which to break for lunch. There's plenty to tempt you, including the big brasserie buzz of **Alcazar** (▷ 144) or the hip fusion cuisine of **Ze Kitchen Galerie** (▷ 151)—both innovative and convivial lunchtime retreats.

Afternoon

Follow rue Dauphine to the **Pont Neuf** (▷ 74), crossing to the Île de la Cité to soak up the sun in the beautiful **square du Vert-Galant** (▷ 75), a tiny park on the island's western tip that offers wonderful views along the Seine. Afterwards, skirt the Île's north bank past the brooding bulk of the **Conciergerie** (▷ 18–19), a former royal palace, fortress and prison. Like the church of **Sainte-Chapelle** (▷ 56–57), it now forms part of the Palais de Justice. Slow the pace to admire the colors of the **Marché aux Fleurs** (▷ 127) before turning down rue de la Cité to reach the cathedral of **Notre-Dame** (▷ 44–45).

Late afternoon

Visiting the cathedral is free, but leave the interior for another day. Instead, admire the flying buttresses from outside and find the small copper Point Zero des Routes de France, from where all French map distances are measured.

Evening

The soft light of evening casts a particularly alluring spell over the **Île Saint-Louis** (▷ 68), for many visitors one of Paris's most romantic corners. Stroll its embankments to enjoy views of Notre-Dame and the Seine before crossing back to the Left Bank for dinner at **La Tour d'Argent** (▷ 151).

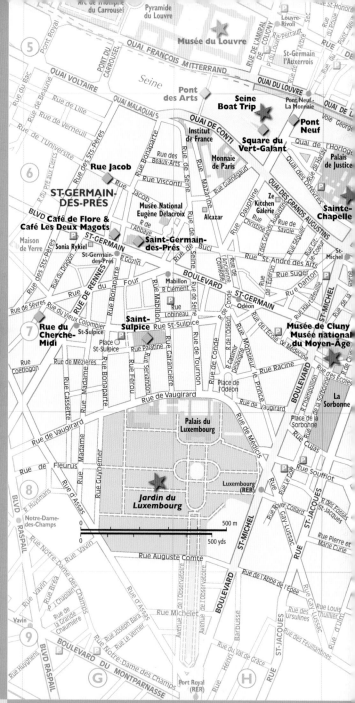

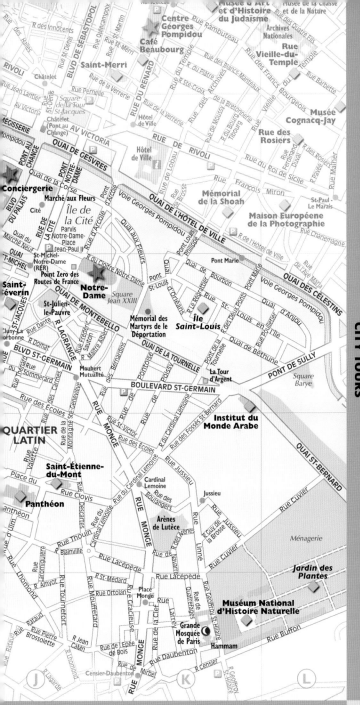

Latin Quarter, St-Germain and Islands
Quick Reference Guide

Conciergerie (▷ 18)
Part medieval palace, part prison, this austere place preserves poignant memories of the victims of the French Revolution, including Marie-Antoinette.

Jardin du Luxembourg (▷ 24)
The epitome of French landscaping, this garden was commissioned by Marie de Médicis in 1615 and designed to remind her of her childhood Florentine home.

Musée de Cluny – Musée national du Moyen-Âge (▷ 30)
A turreted 15th-century mansion provides an appropriate setting for the national collection of medieval and Gothic art.

Notre-Dame (▷ 44)
Spot the gargoyles and admire the French Gothic architecture of this famous cathedral, part of UNESCO's "Paris, Banks of the Seine" World Heritage site.

Sainte-Chapelle (▷ 56)
Hidden within the Palais de Justice is a delicate late Gothic gem: Louis IX's soaring royal chapel, with a star-studded roof and breathtaking stained glass.

Seine Boat Trip (▷ 58)
Your feet will appreciate the rest as you watch the most important sights of Paris float gently by on a romantic one-hour boat trip along the River Seine.

CITY TOURS

CITY TOURS

Marais and Bastille

Contemporary art meets high fashion in Paris's trendiest district, yet alongside the *branché* (hippest) boutiques and bars the Marais preserves magnificent architecture and is the heart of the city's Jewish life.

Morning
Start with a late breakfast on the terrace at the chic **Café Beaubourg** (▷ 66) and ponder the audacious design of the **Centre Georges Pompidou** (▷ 16–17), which caused quite a stir with its exposed ductwork and glass-roofed escalators when it opened in 1977. Today isn't the day to visit; instead, admire the jaunty Fontaine Stravinsky before walking the length of the museum, turning right into rue Rambuteau to reach the **Musée d'Art et d'Histoire du Judaïsme** (▷ 69) on rue du Temple. Housed in a grand 17th-century mansion or *hôtel particulier*, the museum documents European Jewish history and art from the Middle Ages onward.

Late morning
Rue Rambuteau runs into rue des Francs-Bourgeois, graced by more aristocratic town houses. Turn left up **rue Vieille-du-Temple** (▷ 75) to discover some of the Marais' hip designer stores, including **Vanessa Bruno** (▷ 129) at No.100, now a temple to shopping. Turn right into rue Debelleyme and right again to reach the **Musée Picasso** (▷ 38–39), housed in another mansion, the elegant Hôtel Salé. Continue along rue Thorigny to rue Elzévir, where the 16th-century Hôtel Donon houses the **Musée Cognacq-Jay** (▷ 70), whose 18th-century paintings and *objets d'art* were assembled by the owner of the Samaritaine department store. Back on rue des Francs-Bourgeois, the Hôtel Carnavalet also dates from the 16th century and comprises one half of Paris's splendid museum of local history, the **Musée Carnavalet** (▷ 70). Admire the exterior architecture (the interior is currently closed for renovations).

Lunch

If the Marais's trendy shops have drained your funds, the inexpensive Jewish restaurants along **rue des Rosiers** (▷ 75) will be a welcome sight. **L'As du Fallafel** (▷ 145) at No. 34 is generally reckoned to serve the best falafel (mashed chickpeas formed into a ball and deep fried) in the city, but don't come here on Saturday—it's closed.

Afternoon

Retrace your steps to rue des Francs-Bourgeois, continuing as far as **place des Vosges** (▷ 52–53). This beautiful formal square dates from the early 17th century and is the best preserved in Paris; in the southeast corner, Victor Hugo's house is now a museum. Rue de Birague leads from the south side of the square to busy rue Saint-Antoine; to the left is the place de la Bastille, former site of the infamous prison and now dominated by the ultramodern **Opéra Bastille** (▷ 138). To the right, the Hôtel de Béthune-Sully is among the most magnificent of all the Marais's mansions; you can't visit the interior—now occupied by the Ministry of Culture—but you can admire the court and elegant garden. Continue along rue Saint-Antoine and rue François-Miron to reach the **Mémorial de la Shoah** (▷ 69), on rue Geoffroy l'Asnier—a somber counterpoint to the Musée d'Art et d'Histoire du Judaïsme.

Dinner

Bofinger (▷ 146) is one of Paris's most historic brasseries and a memorable spot for dinner. Afterward, stay in the Marais for a drink in one of the area's lively cafés and bars—many of them popular with the city's LGBTQ community.

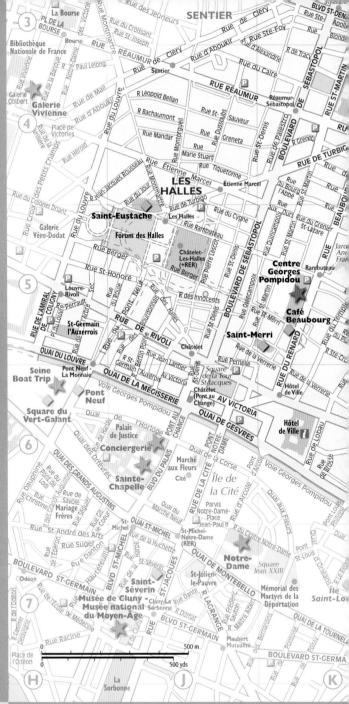

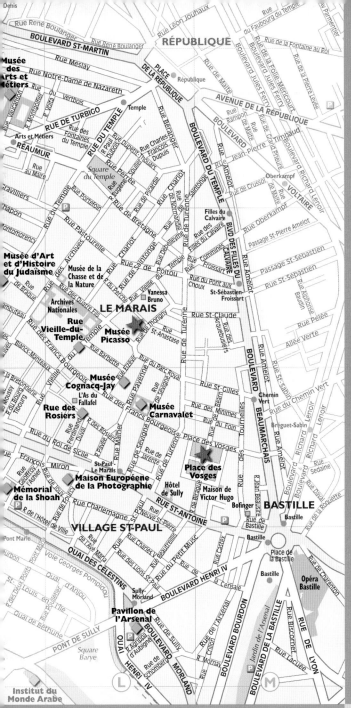

Marais and Bastille
Quick Reference Guide

 SIGHTS AND EXPERIENCES

Centre Georges Pompidou (▷ 16)

The museum houses the large national collection of modern and contemporary art, from fauvism, cubism and surrealism to Pop Art and works by the stars of this art scene. The building includes a library, cinema, bookshops and a chic restaurant.

Musée Picasso (▷ 38)

Some 500 works by Picasso are displayed in this historic Marais mansion, following a thorough refurbishment by architect Jean-François Bodin that has tripled the exhibition area and improved access for visitors with disabilities. It boasts one of the world's finest collections of work by the artist.

Place des Vosges (▷ 52)

Dating from 1612 and built on the site of a 14th-century royal palace that was abandoned and demolished by Catherine de Médici after her husband Henri II died there, this handsome square of arcaded houses overlooks a central garden. Famous former residents include Victor Hugo.

Louvre and Champs-Élysées

Dress to impress for this route through the very heart of Paris, where iconic landmarks and glamorous designer shopping ensure there's plenty of interest along the way.

Morning

Start with a late breakfast on the terrace of the **Café Marly** (▷ 146) at the **Louvre** (▷ 32–33). You'll probably want to set aside another day to see the collection but this is a fine vantage point from which to admire the splendid setting and the audacity of I.M. Pei's modernist glass pyramid. Cross the busy place du Carrousel du Louvre to reach the Arc de Triomphe du Carrousel—not the famous triumphal arch but a smaller version, Roman in its inspiration and built in 1805 to celebrate Napoleon's victories. Beyond it, there's a dramatic view along Paris's monumental axis—west through the **Jardin des Tuileries** (▷ 26–27), across the **place de la Concorde** (▷ 50–51) and up the avenue des Champs-Élysées to the Arc de Triomphe and the distant **Grande Arche** (▷ 76) at La Défense. Paris's most central park, the Jardin des Tuileries has been a UNESCO World Heritage Site since 1991. Two galleries—the **Orangerie** (▷ 71–72) and **Jeu de Paume** (▷ 51)—offer an excellent excuse to linger a while.

Mid-morning

Leave the Jardin des Tuileries at the Carrousel du Louvre exit and cross rue de Rivoli, walking straight ahead along the avenue de l'Opera. Turn right into rue Richelieu and immediately on your right is the ornate facade of the **Comédie-Française** (▷ 136), famed for its classical theater. Behind the building, discover the historic gardens of the **Domaine National du Palais Royal** (▷ 66). Return to Avenue de l'Opera and turn right into rue Saint-Honoré to browse and window-shop. No. 233 is home to luggage-maker **Goyard** (▷ 126). At the corner of place Vendôme, look right to see one of the most elegant squares in the city with a 44m (144ft) bronze column in its center.

Beyond rue Royale, rue Saint-Honoré becomes rue du Faubourg Saint-Honoré, home to the Élysée palace—official residence of the French president—the **Grand Musée du Parfum** (▷ 68), and to some of Paris's most chic designer boutiques. Avenue Matignon continues the luxury theme but with fine art galleries and antiques dealers instead of fashion.

Lunch
Take a table on the terrace at **L'Avenue** (▷ 145) on avenue Montaigne for good bistro food and some first class people watching, this is Parisian chic at it's best.

Afternoon
The window-shopping shifts up a gear on the far side of the Rond Point des Champs-Élysées along avenue Montaigne. Here, **Dior** (▷ 125) and **Chanel** (▷ 124) both have splendid flagship stores in which to lose half a day, and the array of designer labels is enough to constitute a serious hazard to your bank balance. Turn right off avenue Montaigne up rue François 1er to reach the broad avenue des Champs-Élysées, Paris's most famous boulevard. It ends at place de l'Étoile, dominated by the stately bulk of the **Arc de Triomphe** (▷ 14–15). Quite aside from its significance as a national monument, the Arc also makes an excellent platform for views across the city.

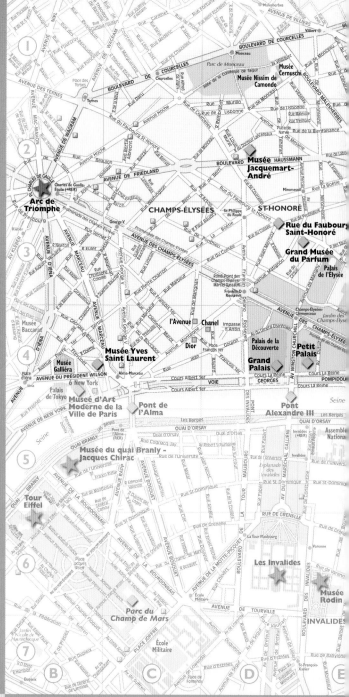

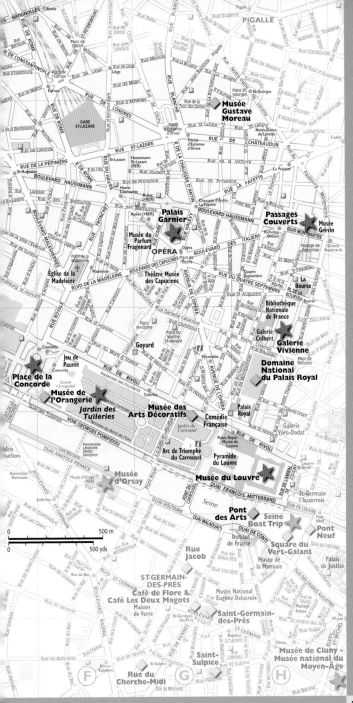

PIGALLE

GARE ST-LAZARE

Musée Gustave Moreau

Palais Garnier

Musée du Parfum Fragonard

OPÉRA

Passages Couverts

Musée Grévin

Église de la Madeleine

Théâtre Musée des Capucines

La Bourse

Bibliothèque Nationale de France

Galerie Colbert

Galerie Vivienne

Goyard

Domaine National du Palais Royal

Jeu de Paume

Place de la Concorde

Musée de l'Orangerie

Jardin des Tuileries

Musée des Arts Décoratifs

Comédie Française

Palais Royal

Galerie Véro-Dodat

Arc de Triomphe du Carrousel

Pyramide du Louvre

Musée d'Orsay

Musée du Louvre

Pont des Arts

Seine Boat Trip

Pont Neuf

Square du Vert-Galant

Palais de Justice

Rue Jacob

ST-GERMAIN-DES-PRÉS

Café de Flore & Café Les Deux Magots

Maison de Verre

Musée National Eugène Delacroix

Saint-Germain-des-Prés

Saint-Sulpice

Musée de Cluny – Musée national du Moyen-Âge

Rue du Cherche-Midi

0 ___ 500 m
0 ___ 500 yds

F   G   H

Louvre and Champs-Élysées
Quick Reference Guide

TOP 25 SIGHTS AND EXPERIENCES

Arc de Triomphe (▷ 14)
With 12 of Haussmann's avenues radiating from it, this arch is the focus of national pride and a memorial to France's war dead, with a Memorial Flame at its base.

Galerie Vivienne and the Passages Couverts (▷ 20)
A network of 19th-century shopping arcades allows you to stroll and people-watch under cover.

Jardin des Tuileries (▷ 26)
First laid out in the 16th century, this is one of the most popular parks for Parisians. It is a delightful place in which to stop and relax.

Musée du Louvre (▷ 32)
The world's largest museum is a dazzling experience, from the modernist glass pyramid over its entrance to the world-famous treasures it contains.

Palais Garnier (▷ 46)
Charles Garnier's wedding cake of a building is as sumptuous as an opera house should be, with a foyer and grand staircase every bit as majestic as the auditorium itself.

Place de la Concorde (▷ 50)
A maelstrom of traffic today, this vast open space was the site of the gruesome guillotine and many public executions during the French Revolution.

CITY TOURS

Montmartre

There's art, raffish nightlife, picturesque views and stepped streets in this remarkably village-like corner of the city.

Morning

Wear comfortable shoes—the route is mostly downhill and avoids steps as far as possible, but this is still the highest point in the city; the slopes can be steep and the streets are cobbled in places. Take the Métro to Abbesses station; it's the city's deepest, with an original art nouveau canopy. Window-shop your way from **place des Abbesses** (▷ 73–74) past small boutiques in rue Yvonne le Tac and rue Tardieu to reach the funicular. One of the area's celebrated stepped streets runs parallel to it, but the railway is easier on your feet. Journey's end is the distinctive, white hilltop basilica of **Sacré-Cœur** (▷ 54–55). It's one of Paris's most visited attractions and the crush inside can sometimes mar the experience. What doesn't disappoint is the breathtaking view over the city—whether from the dome or from the terrace in front of the church.

Late morning

Follow rue du Cardinal Guibert along the side of the church, braving the busy rue Chevalier de la Barre to reach calmer, prettier rue Cortot. Here, the **Musée de Montmartre** (▷ 71) documents the history and artistic associations of the area, which in the 19th century became a popular place of entertainment. Continue along rue Cortot to the junction with rue des Saules—if you haven't already caught a glimpse of Montmartre's vineyard, it's just downhill to the right. Turn uphill along rue des Saules then left into rue Norvins to reach busy **place du Tertre**, famous for its portrait painters.

Lunch

This is an unashamedly touristy part of Montmartre, with no shortage of places to eat, though there are many cafés with daily menus of variable quality; **Au Clair de la Lune** (▷ 145) in rue Poulbot is one of the nicest options, tucked away off place du Tertre. In summer, arrive early to make sure you get one of the tables outside.

Afternoon

From rue Poulbot, turn left down rue Norvins to reach the Radet, the first of Montmartre's windmills, at the top of rue Lepic; there were once 14 but now this and the nearby Blute Fin are the last survivors. Together they constitute the **Moulin de la Galette**, which during its time as a dance hall was painted by Renoir. It is now a restaurant. Continue downhill on rue Lepic, turning sharply right at its junction with rue des Abbesses to reach the **Cimetière de Montmartre** (▷ 66), where the roll call of famous names rivals that of Père Lachaise.

Evening

Rue des Abbesses and the surrounding streets hum with life in the evening; catch a film at **Studio 28** (▷ 139), enjoy dinner at **Seb'on** (▷ 151) or dinner and a show at **Michou** (▷ 138). Later and much livelier nightlife—from rock concerts to discos and sleazy sex clubs—is found at the foot of rue des Martyrs on place Pigalle and boulevard de Clichy, the latter dominated by the famous **Moulin Rouge** (▷ 138) club.

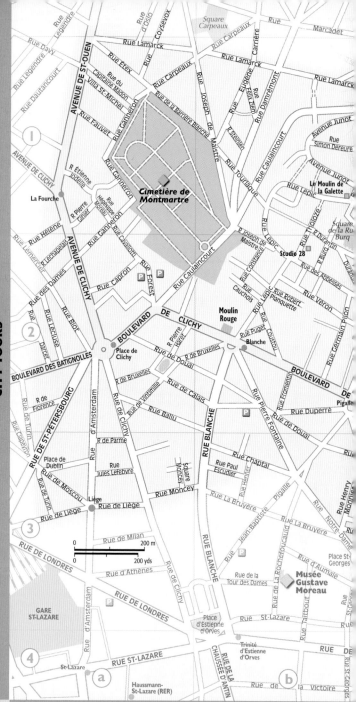

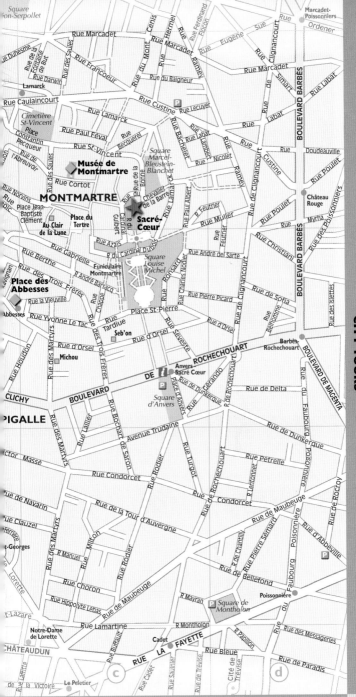

Montmartre Quick Reference Guide

TOP 25 SIGHTS AND EXPERIENCES

Sacré-Cœur (▷ 54)
Neo-Romanesque and Byzantine in style, the white basilica of Sacré-Cœur is one of the most familiar features of the Parisian skyline, looking down on the city from its lofty hilltop perch. Built as a memorial to the dead of the Franco-Prussian war and Paris Commune, it wasn't completed until the eve of World War I and was only consecrated in 1919. Its lovely stained-glass windows were destroyed during World War II and restored afterwards.

MORE TO SEE	64

Cimetière de Montmartre
Musée de Montmartre

Place des Abbesses

The interior of Sacré-Cœur

SHOP 118

Books and CDs
Librairie des Abbesses
Clothes and Hats
Petit Bateau

Concept Store
Le Sept Cinq
Markets
Marché Barbès
Marché de la rue Lepic

ENTERTAINMENT 130

Cinemas
Studio 28
Clubs
Michou

Contemporary Music
La Boule Noire/La Cigale
Divan du Monde
Shows
Moulin Rouge

EAT 140

French-Bistro
Au Virage Lepic
Le Progrès
Seb'on
French-Regional
Au Clair de la Lune

Italian/Mediterranean
Pink Mamma
Organic
Rose Bakery

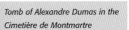

Tomb of Alexandre Dumas in the Cimetière de Montmartre

Montmartre

Farther Afield

Louis XIV's palace at Versailles is one excursion not to miss, while more offbeat charm is to be found in the outer *arrondissements* of the city's north and east.

DAY 1
Morning
Take RER Line C to Versailles Rive Gauche and then stroll the short distance to the **Château de Versailles** (▷ 62–63). Try for an early start—the château opens at 9—and buy your ticket online to avoid a long wait in line. Start with the Grands Appartements: Admire the bombastic painted ceiling of the exquisite Hall of Mirrors, which celebrates Louis XIV's military campaigns, before visiting the King's Apartment.

Lunch
If you're visiting at the weekend between April and October, exit into the gardens before midday to catch the Grandes Eaux fountains performing to music; they do the same again from 3.30 to 5.30. Afterwards, stroll down to the Grand Canal where there are formal and informal lunch options—La Flottille (tel 01 39 51 41 58, laflottille.fr) has a garden terrace by the waterside.

Afternoon
Follow the route marked on the free map to reach the **Petit Trianon** (▷ 63). Closely associated with Marie-Antoinette, this country estate is for many the highlight of a visit to Versailles. Explore the twee Hameau de la Reine—a play village built for the queen's amusement—before continuing through formal gardens to reach the **Grand Trianon** (▷ 63), the colonnaded marble palace where Louis XIV enjoyed trysts with his mistress, Madame de Montespan.

DAY 2
Morning
Another early start, this time for a weekend stroll through the **Marché aux Puces de Saint-Ouen** (▷ 28–29)—Paris's most famous flea market. Take Métro Line 4 to Porte de Clignancourt and cross under the Périphérique to get there by 10. Fortify yourself with coffee from one of the cafés along rue des Rosiers and pick up a free map from the tourist office at 7 impasse Simon by the Marché Paul Bert to navigate your way. Take a couple of hours to appreciate the sheer variety on offer, from secondhand clothes to elegant art deco furniture and fine art.

Lunch
Take the Métro to Barbès–Rochechouart, change to Line 2 (direction: Nation) and alight at Stalingrad. Admire the 18th-century Rotonde de la Villette and the views up the canal basin toward **Parc de la Villette** (▷ 76) before climbing hilly avenue Sécretan. Assemble a picnic from the covered market and shops here. Eat it in the **Parc des Buttes Chaumont** (▷ 76) at the top of the hill—if you're lucky, you might get one of its hillocks to yourself.

Afternoon
Descend avenue Mathurin Moreau to Colonel Fabien station. Take the Métro to Père Lachaise—there's a gate into the **Cimetière du Père Lachaise** (▷ 48–49) directly opposite, but the main entrance is farther along boulevard de Ménilmontant. Pick up a map to find the most-visited graves, including those of Oscar Wilde, Édith Piaf and Jim Morrison, but be sure to admire the extraordinary architecture of the many tombs, too.

Early evening
Stay in the area for an apéritif or relaxed early dinner in the very vibrant rue Oberkampf. For a contemporary French bistro experience, head to dinner at **Septime** (▷ 151) close by on rue Charonne.

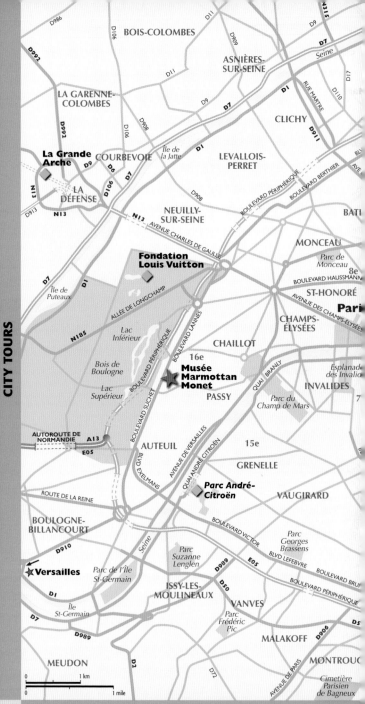

BOIS-COLOMBES

D986

D106

D11

D9

D9

N315

D7

Seine

ASNIÈRES-SUR-SEINE

D992

LA GARENNE-COLOMBES

D11

D9

D7

D1

RUE MARTRE

D17

D110

CLICHY

D911

D992

D908

D106

D106

La Grande Arche

D9

COURBEVOIE

Île de la Jatte

LEVALLOIS-PERRET

BLV

N13

D6

D7

LA DÉFENSE

D106

AVE

BOULEVARD BERTHIER

D913

N13

N13

NEUILLY-SUR-SEINE

D908

BATI

AVENUE CHARLES DE GAULLE

BOULEVARD PÉRIPHÉRIQUE

MONCEAU

Parc de Monceau

8e

Fondation Louis Vuitton

BOULEVARD HAUSSMANN

D7

D1

ST-HONORÉ

Île de Puteaux

ALLÉE DE LONGCHAMP

AVENUE DES CHAMPS-ELYSÉES

Pari

CHAMPS-ÉLYSÉES

N185

Lac Inférieur

BOULEVARD PÉRIPHÉRIQUE

BOULEVARD LANNES

CHAILLOT

16e

Musée Marmottan Monet

Esplanad des Invalio

Bois de Boulogne

QUAI BRANLY

INVALIDES

Lac Supérieur

BOULEVARD SUCHET

PASSY

Parc du Champ de Mars

7

AUTOROUTE DE NORMANDIE

A13

E05

AUTEUIL

15e

AVENUE DE VERSAILLES

QUAI ANDRÉ CITROËN

GRENELLE

BOULEVARD EXELMANS

ROUTE DE LA REINE

Parc André-Citroën

VAUGIRARD

BOULOGNE-BILLANCOURT

BOULEVARD VICTOR

Parc Georges Brassens

D910

Seine

Parc Suzanne Lenglen

D989

E05

BLVD LEFEBVRE

BOULEVARD BRUI

Versailles

Parc de l'Île St-Germain

D50

BOULEVARD PÉRIPHÉRIQUE

D1

ISSY-LES-MOULINEAUX

VANVES

DS

Île St-Germain

Parc Frédéric Pic

D906

D7

D989

MEUDON

D2

D72

MALAKOFF

MONTROUC

AVENUE DE PARIS

Cimetière Parisien de Bagneux

0   1 km

0   1 mile

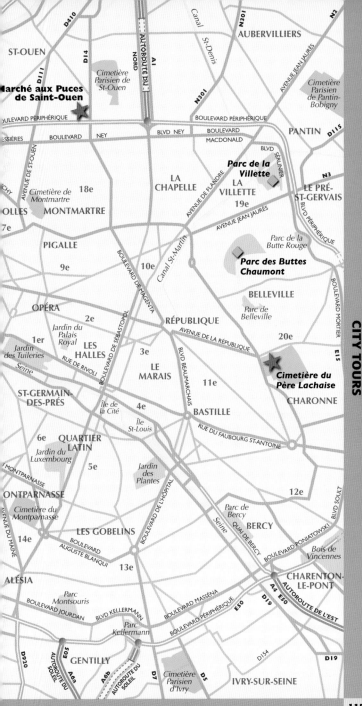

ST-OUEN

Cimetière
Parisien de
St-Ouen

Marché aux Puces
de Saint-Ouen

AUBERVILLIERS

Canal

St-Denis

AVENUE JEAN JAURÈS

Cimetière
Parisien
de Pantin-
Bobigny

BOULEVARD PÉRIPHÉRIQUE

BOULEVARD PÉRIPHÉRIQUE

PANTIN

BOULEVARD NEY

BLVD NEY

BOULEVARD
MACDONALD

BLVD SERURIER

Parc de la
Villette

LA
CHAPELLE

LA
VILLETTE

19e

LE PRÉ-
ST-GERVAIS

Cimetière de
Montmartre

18e

AVENUE DE FLANDRE

AVENUE JEAN JAURÈS

MONTMARTRE

BOULEVARD PÉRIPHÉRIQUE

Parc de la
Butte Rouge

PIGALLE

9e

10e

Canal St-Martin

Parc des Buttes
Chaumont

BELLEVILLE

Parc de
Belleville

BOULEVARD DE MAGENTA

BOULEVARD MORTIER

OPÉRA

2e

RÉPUBLIQUE

AVENUE DE LA RÉPUBLIQUE

20e

Jardin du
Palais
Royal

1er

LES
HALLES

3e

BOULEVARD DE SÉBASTOPOL

BLVD BEAUMARCHAIS

Cimetière du
Père Lachaise

Jardin
des Tuileries

RUE DE RIVOLI

LE
MARAIS

11e

CHARONNE

Seine

ST-GERMAIN-
DES-PRÉS

4e

Île de
la Cité

Île
St-Louis

BASTILLE

RUE DU FAUBOURG ST-ANTOINE

6e

QUARTIER
LATIN

Jardin du
Luxembourg

5e

Jardin
des
Plantes

BOULEVARD DE L'HÔPITAL

12e

BLVD SOULT

MONTPARNASSE

Cimetière du
Montparnasse

LES GOBELINS

Parc de
Bercy

BERCY

QUAI DE BERCY

Seine

BOULEVARD PONIATOWSKI

Bois de
Vincennes

14e

BOULEVARD
AUGUSTE BLANQUI

13e

BOULEVARD MASSÉNA

CHARENTON-
LE-PONT

AUTOROUTE DE L'EST

ALÉSIA

Parc
Montsouris

BOULEVARD JOURDAN

BLVD KELLERMANN

BOULEVARD PÉRIPHÉRIQUE

Parc
Kellermann

GENTILLY

AUTOROUTE DU SOLEIL

Cimetière
Parisien
d'Ivry

IVRY-SUR-SEINE

SIGHTS AND EXPERIENCES

Marché aux Puces de Saint-Ouen (▷ 28)

The sprawling, 7ha (15-acre) Marché aux Puces de Saint-Ouen is not one market but a series of market buildings, arcades, stalls and individual dealers. Together they create an enjoyable way to spend a weekend morning mingling with the locals.

Musée Marmottan Monet (▷ 34)

This 19th-century mansion is an elegant setting for a truly mesmerizing collection of Impressionist paintings, including Monet's memorable and world-renowned canvases of dappled irises, wisteria and water lilies from his last years at Giverny.

Père Lachaise (▷ 48)

The chance to see the tombs of literary, musical and artistic greats—including Frederick Chopin, Marcel Proust and Oscar Wilde—is what draws many visitors to this historic cemetery in the east of the city. The wonderful architecture of its myriad tombs and vaults repays languid exploration.

Versailles (▷ 62)

The grandeur of the Sun King, Louis XIV, survives in swaggering stone form at the Château de Versailles, but the complex also offers more intimate glimpses of royal life at the estates of Grand and Petit Trianon. Despite the crowds, this rural idyll makes for a perfect day away from the city rush.

Modern design on a huge scale, La Grand Arche

Shop

Whether you're looking for the best local products, a department store or a quirky boutique, you'll find them all in Paris. In this section shops are listed alphabetically.

SHOP

Introduction

One of the world's shopping capitals, Paris is not all about luxury designer stores. Don't forget the individual shops, inexpensive chain stores, big and small flea markets and everything in between.

The Capital of Fashion

Narrow rue du Faubourg Saint-Honoré and broad, stately avenue Montaigne are the most prestigious fashion addresses in the city—the places to go for couture, luxury and high price tags, or simply for a spot of *lèche-vitrines* (window-shopping) past the beautiful displays. In these streets you'll find the top names—Gucci, Roberto Cavalli and Prada. Rue de la Paix glitters with names, including Cartier and Van Cleef et Arpels. To the north are the great Belle Époque department stores of boulevard Haussmann, Galeries Lafayette and Printemps, complete with English-speaking guides on hand.

Nip across the Seine to Saint-Germain-des-Prés for fashion with flair alongside fine art and antiques and, farther south, the city's oldest department store, Le Bon Marché Rive Gauche (▷ 124), at 24 rue de Sèvres.

The Capital of Chic

Be sure not to miss the historic *arrondissements* between the Louvre and Bastille. Fashion has colonized the area around place des Victoires in the 1st *arrondissement* with

GOURMET PICNICS

There isn't a word for delicatessen in French. A *charcuterie* is a pork butcher and a *traiteur*, a caterer or a shop selling ready-cooked dishes. The two are closely related and are often combined. Inside, glass cabinets or counters display dozens of exquisite freshly prepared salads, such as grated carrot, paper-thin slices of cucumber, aubergines (eggplant) and mushrooms, as well as meat pies and spicy sausages, garlic, bean-and-pork stew and a gourmet mix of cooked meats.

Clockwise from top: Tasty choices at Le Bon Marché Rive Gauche; the enticing facade to some of the city's chic shops; sweet treats from Stohrer chocolate

Christian Louboutin and Stella McCartney opening boutiques in the Palais Royal; farther east, rue Étienne-Marcel is good for youth-oriented labels, while rue Vieille-du-Temple in the Marais is a must-see for its mix of small boutiques and intriguing concept stores.

Out of the Rain

In the Sentier and Opéra districts, explore delightful, shop-lined 19th-century arcades, full of quirky and interesting small boutiques that make them an excellent place to linger if the weather is wet.

Buy the Best

Seek out great French flair and quality, not just in fashion but also in high-quality cookware—Le Creuset saucepans, Sabatier knives, kitchen gadgets that actually work, such as a Peugeot peppermill—and in stylish children's and baby clothes. For epicurean delights try exquisite prepared foods from Fauchon (▷ 125) or La Grande Épicerie at Le Bon Marché Rive Gauche, handmade chocolates and fine wines, which all make tempting buys.

Down to Earth

If luxury and high fashion are not for you there are bargains to be had, so join the locals at the legendary flea markets, starting with Marché aux Puces de Saint-Ouen (▷ 28–29).

SHOP

WHAT'S WHAT

Boulangeries sell baguettes, and more besides; try the *ficelle*, a thinner, finer loaf, or *pain au levain*, delicious sourdough bread. And then there are the croissants, *ordinaire* or *au beurre* (with butter). *Pâtisseries* sell pastries and tarts. *Charcuteries* sell cold meats, snails, cheese, truffles, wines, caviar and more. *Parfumeries* can stock solely French perfume but some sell cosmetics and soaps, too. *Bouquinistes* sell used books, prints, posters and postcards.

---

and pastry shop; the latest shoe trends to tempt shoppers; a cheese made in France's Auvergne region, Bleu d'Auvergne, for sale in the city

Directory

Shopping A–Z

À LA MÈRE DE FAMILLE
lameredefamille.com

This original 18th-century grocery shop has shelves laden with imaginatively created chocolates, jams and unusual groceries. Beautifully packaged, these edible treats make great presents to take back home. There are ten stores around the city.

🔲 H2 ✉ 33–35 rue du Faubourg Montmartre, 75009 ☎ 01 47 70 83 69 🕐 Mon–Sat 9.30–8, Sun 10–7.30 🚇 Le Peletier, Cadet

AGNÈS B
europe.agnesb.com

Agnès B's fashion is the epitome of young Parisian chic: sharply cut clothes with original details. French-born Agnès worked her way up from assistant fashion editor to own-name label, and her clothes are still made in France.

🔲 J4 ✉ 6 rue du Jour, 75001 ☎ 01 45 08 56 56 🕐 May–Sep Mon–Sat 10.30–7.30; Oct–Apr Mon–Fri 10.30–7.30, Sat 10.30–8 🚇 Les Halles

ARTAZART
artazart.com

Located on the banks of the Canal Saint-Martin, this bookshop specializes in design, architecture, photography and fashion. A small gallery shows work by up-and-coming artists.

🔲 M7 ✉ 83 quai de Valmy, 75010 ☎ 01 40 40 24 03 🕐 Mon–Fri 10.30–7.30, Sat 11–7.30, Sun 1–7.30 🚇 Jacques Bonsergent, République

AU BAIN MARIE
aubainmarie.fr

Ceramic artist Aude Clément founded this now renowned emporium to sell her own

WINDOW-SHOPPING

Some Parisian streets do not fit any convenient label and so make for intriguing window-shopping. Try rue Jean-Jacques Rousseau and Passage Véro-Dodat, rue Saint-Roch, rue Monsieur-le-Prince and parallel rue de l'Odéon, rue Saint-Sulpice, rue des Francs-Bourgeois and rue du Pont-Louis-Philippe or rue de la Roquette. For luxury goods, take a stroll along the rue du Faubourg-Saint-Honoré.

hand-crafted ranges of tableware and practical objets d'art. The impressive showroom now sells a specially chosen selection from other ceramic artists.

🔲 G6 ✉ 56 rue de l'Université, 75007 ☎ 01 42 71 08 69 🕐 Tue–Sat 11–7 🚇 Solferino

AZZEDINE ALAÏA
alaia.fr

Alaïa, an artistic genius of the fashion world, is a Tunisian-born fashion designer with an eye for "feminine Hollywood" glamor, and the showroom is the place to come for his signature silhouette-hugging dresses.

🔲 K6 ✉ 7 rue de Moussy, 75004 ☎ 01 42 72 30 69 🕐 Mon–Sat 10–7 🚇 Hôtel de Ville

BHV
bhv.fr

You can't buy shoes in this department store, but otherwise it's famous for having everything you'll ever need, from baby clothes to an electrical transformer. You can even get your watch battery replaced should you need to.

🔲 K6 ✉ 52 rue de Rivoli, 75004 ☎ 09 77 40 14 00 🕐 Mon–Sat 9.30–8, Sun 11–7 🚇 Hôtel de Ville

SHOP

LE BON MARCHÉ RIVE GAUCHE

lebonmarche.com

Classy goods abound in this Left Bank store. Don't miss the beauty shop on the ground floor or the excellent food hall, La Grande Épicerie, in an adjoining building, which stocks delicacies from all over the world.

➕ F7 ✉ 24 rue de Sèvres, 75007 ☎ 01 44 39 80 00 🕙 Mon–Wed, Fri–Sat 10–8, Thu 10–8.45, Sun 11–8 Ⓜ Sèvres–Babylone

CARTIER

cartier.fr

This is the traditional Paris home of the exclusive jeweler, known the world over, selling contemporary and vintage jewelry, watches, leather goods and perfumes. There's another branch right around the corner on place Vendôme.

➕ G3 ✉ 13 rue de la Paix, 75002 ☎ 01 58 18 23 00 🕙 Mon–Sat 11–7 Ⓜ Opéra

CHANEL

chanel.com

Chanel's fashion embodies Parisian style. Here, there is everything from fashion to jewelry, leather goods, watches, sunglasses, perfume and beauty products.

➕ D4 ✉ 51 avenue Montaigne, 75008 ☎ 01 40 70 73 00 🕙 Mon–Sat 10–7, Sun 11–7 Ⓜ Franklin D Roosevelt

CHRISTIAN LOUBOUTIN

christianlouboutin.com

A shoe fetishist's dream, Christian Louboutin is the place to go for exquisite women's shoes with glamor and extreme heels.

➕ H5 ✉ 19 rue Jean-Jacques Rousseau 75001 ☎ 0800 94 58 04 🕙 Mon–Sat 10.30–7 Ⓜ Louvre–Rivoli

DEHILLERIN

e-dehillerin.fr

Come here for all your top-end kitchen needs—copper pans, knives, bains-marie, sieves and more. A mail-order service is also available.

➕ H4 ✉ 18–20 rue Coquillière, 75001 ☎ 01 42 36 53 13 🕙 Mon 9–12.30, 2–6, Tue–Sat 9–6 Ⓜ Les Halles, Louvre–Rivoli

DETAILLE

detaille.com

This Paris beauty shop, which celebrated its centenary in 2005, was opened by the Countess de Presle, one of the first people in Paris to own a car. She created the store's best-selling antipollution face cream, Baume Automobile.

➕ G2 ✉ 10 rue Saint-Lazare, 75009 ☎ 01 48 78 68 50 🕙 Tue–Sat 11–2, 3–7 Ⓜ Notre-Dame-de-Lorette

DIDIER LUDOT

didierludot.fr

Good quality pre-owned vintage designer clothes (by the likes of

Chanel, Dior, Balmain, Givenchy and Lanvin) and classic Hermès handbags are sold at this shop in a picturesque location.

⊞ H4 ⊠ 20–24 Galerie Montpensier, 75001 ☎ 01 42 96 06 56 🕙 Mon–Sat 10.30–7 🚇 Palais-Royal–Musée du Louvre

DIOR

dior.com

Dior's historic headquarters sells everything from the ready-to-wear collection to menswear, jewelry and accessories. The store offers the current season range, including classic evening wear.

⊞ C4 ⊠ 30 avenue Montaigne, 75008 ☎ 01 40 73 73 73 🕙 Mon–Sat 10–7, Sun 11–7 🚇 Franklin D Roosevelt

DIPTYQUE

diptyqueparis.fr

Diptyque sells the ultimate in crafted candles, in a choice of 48 exquisite scents. There's also a divine range of eau de cologne.

⊞ J7 ⊠ 34 boulevard Saint-Germain, 75005 ☎ 01 43 26 77 44 🕙 Mon–Sat 10–7 🚇 Maubert–Mutualité

DROUOT RICHELIEU

drouot.com

Paris's main auction rooms are where anything from a Persian carpet to a Louis XV commode may come under the hammer.

⊞ H2 ⊠ 9 rue Drouot, 75009 ☎ 01 48 00 20 20 🕙 Mon–Fri 11–6 (most auctions start at 2pm); closed Aug 🚇 Richelieu–Drouot

FAUCHON

fauchon.com

Paris's most renowned *épicerie* is a visual and gastronomic feast for foodies, complete with an excellent pâtisserie, a deli and a wine shop in imposing premises close to the Madeleine.

⊞ F3 ⊠ 30 place de la Madeleine, 75008 ☎ 01 70 39 38 02 🕙 Mon–Sat 10–8, boulangerie Mon–Sat 8–7 🚇 Madeleine

FORUM DES HALLES

forumdeshalles.com

Partially underground, this shopping complex is the biggest in central Paris and contains a few surprises —including a Muji store— among its predominantly mainstream fashion brands. The complex has also benefited from a multi-million dollar refit.

⊞ J5 ⊠ 1–7 rue Pierre-Lescot, 75001 ☎ 01 44 76 87 08 🕙 Mon–Sat 10–8 🚇 Châtelet-Les Halles

FREE'P'STAR

freepstar.com

There's a wonderful rummage-sale ambience at this popular second-hand clothes shop in the Marais, where the styles range from leopardskin to military surplus.

⊞ K6 ⊠ 61 rue de la Verrerie, 75004 ☎ 01 42 78 00 76 🕙 Mon–Sat 11–8.30, Sun 12–8.30 🚇 Hôtel de Ville

Vintage fashion at Didier Ludot

GALERIE CAPTIER

galeriecaptier.com

The antique Chinese and Japanese furniture (17th to 19th century) and beautiful old Japanese screens sold here have been chosen by owners Bernard and Sylvie Captier, who regularly travel to Asia to search out exotic and refined works of art.

➕ G6 ✉ 33 rue de Beaune, 75007 ☎ 01 42 61 00 57 🕐 Mon 2.30–7, Tue–Sat 11–7 🚇 Rue du Bac

LA GALERIE FAYET

galerie-fayet.com

Owned for many years by the now retired Mr Segas, this quirky shop selling antique walking canes is tucked into one of Paris's attractive and historic 19th-century shopping arcades. The collection has been expanded by the current owners to include a range of high quality umbrellas.

➕ H3 ✉ 34 passage Jouffroy, 75001 ☎ 01 47 70 89 65 🕐 Tue–Sat 10.30am– 12.30pm, 1–7 🚇 Grands Boulevards

DEPARTMENT STORES

Printemps and Galeries Lafayette, in the prestigious boulevard Haussmann, each stock hundreds of brands—from fashion to designer homeware. Printemps (🕐 Mon–Wed, Fri–Sat 9.35–8, Thu 9.35–8.45, Sun 11–7 🚇 Havre-Caumartin) claims to have Europe's largest beauty department. Don't miss the art nouveau stained-glass cupola on the sixth floor of Printemps de la Mode, or the view from the ninth floor of Printemps de la Maison. At Galeries Lafayette (🕐 Mon– Sat 9.30–8.30, Sun 11–7 🚇 Chaussée d'Antin) highlights include the 1912 Byzantine-style glass dome and the Lafayette Gourmet food hall.

GALERIE DE L'OPÉRA DE PARIS

This boutique-bookshop focuses on opera and choreography, with all the latest CDs and books, as well as postcards, posters and gifts. It's also the place to buy a set of opera glasses for the evening performance.

➕ G3 ✉ Opéra Palais Garnier, rue Halévy, 75009 ☎ 01 53 43 03 97 🕐 Daily 10–7.30 🚇 Opéra

GOYARD

goyard.com

Founded in 1792 and in the same premises since 1834, Goyard manufactures and sells some of the world's finest luggage. Beautifully crafted, rugged and a classic statement of style, these trunks and bags are underground style icons.

➕ F4 ✉ 233 rue Saint-Honoré, 75001 ☎ 01 42 60 57 04 🕐 Mon–Sat 10–7 🚇 Concorde, Tuileries

LIBRAIRIE DES ABBESSES

In a city famed for its writers and novelists, independent bookshops are now a rarity, but this is a great little bookshop for those who read French or want to practice. It also sells beautiful art books.

➕ c2 ✉ 30 rue Yvonne le Tac, 75018 ☎ 01 46 06 84 30 🕐 Mon 11–8, Tue–Fri 9.30–8, Sat 10–8, Sun 12–8 🚇 Abbesses

LOUIS VUITTON

louisvuitton.com

The ultimate brand name on the Champs-Élysées and an essential store for all label-concious visitors. Louis Vuitton began his family business in the 1850s and the accessories are still synonymous with quality.

Louis Vuitton on the Champs-Élysées

🟦 C3 ✉ 101 avenue des Champs-Élysées, 75008 ☎ 01 53 57 52 00 🕐 Mon–Sat 10–8, Sun 11–7 Ⓜ George V

MARCHÉ BARBÈS

Come to this colorful market for ethnic wares, scarves, fruit, spices and vegetables. Shop where the locals shop for a taste of Parisian neighborhood banter.
🟦 Off map at d2 ✉ Boulevard de la Chapelle, 75018 🕐 Wed 8–1, Sat 7–3 Ⓜ Barbès–Rochechouart

MARCHÉ AUX FLEURS

Housed in picturesque pavilions, this flower and plant market meets every horticultural need. Thousands of pots are displayed, plus trees and shrubs.
🟦 J6 ✉ Place Louis Lépine, 75004, Île de la Cité 🕐 Mon–Sat 8–7.30 (bird market on Sun) Ⓜ Cité

MARCHÉ DE LA RUE LEPIC

It's up a steep hill but worth the effort to explore this atmospheric street, made famous in the film *Amélie* (2001). The best food shops are from the junction with rue des Abbesses down to boulevard de Clichy.
🟦 b2 ✉ Rue Lepic and rue des Abbesses, 75018 🕐 Most shops open Tue–Sat 9–1, 4–7, Sun 9–1 Ⓜ Abbesses, Blanche

MARIAGE FRÈRES

mariagefreres.com
This teahouse, founded in 1854, offers a choice of hundreds of teas from all over the world, including a selection of exclusive house blends. The company also sells accessories like fine porcelain teapots and cups. There is also a restaurant on-site that serves lunch and afternoon tea.

🟦 K6 ✉ 30 rue du Bourg-Tibourg, 75004 ☎ 01 42 72 28 11 🕐 Daily 10.30–7.30; tea room 12–7 Ⓜ Hôtel de Ville

MERCI

merci-merci.com
One of the most popular concept stores in Paris. Shop with stylish Parisians for an astonishing range of clothing, homewares and decor. There's a used bookstore and three casual eateries on site. It would be easy to browse for hours in this store.
🟦 M5 ✉ 111 Boulevard Beaumarchais, 7003 ☎ 01 42 77 00 33 🕐 Daily 10–7.30 Ⓜ Saint-Sébastien Froissart

NAÏLA DE MONBRISON

Naila-de-monbrison.com
If you are looking for an item of jewelry that isn't mainstream, this store stocks a great choice by a number of contemporary independent designers. The range runs the complete gamut of precious and semi-precious stones, metalwork and glass, and includes some extremely eye-catching pieces.

Flower market on the Île de la Cité

🔲 E5 ✉ 6 rue de Bourgogne, 75007
☎ 01 47 05 11 15 🕒 Mon–Sat 11–1.30,
2.30–7 🚇 Assemble Nationale

PARIS SAINT-GERMAIN STORE
boutiquepsg.fr

Paris may be the city of romance,
but it is its world-famous soccer
team, Paris Saint-Germain (or PSG
as it is more popularly known),
that ignites the passions of Paris's
many soccer fans. This flagship
store sells a wide range of official
merchandise, including replica
shirts, plus a selection of PSG
related memorabilia.

🔲 D3 ✉ 27 ave de Champs-Élysées,
75008 ☎ 0969 32 21 62 🕒 Mon–Sat
10–10, Sun 10–9 🚇 Franklin D Roosevelt

PATRICK ROGER
patrickroger.com

Winner of the prestigious Meilleur
Ouvrier de France (Best Craftsman
in France) for chocolate products,
Patrick Roger is a sculptor of chocolate as well as a chocolate maker.

🔲 H7 ✉ 108 boulevard Saint-Germain,
75006 ☎ 01 43 29 38 42 🕒 Daily 10.30–
7.30 🚇 Odéon

PETIT BATEAU
petit-bateau.com

Every grown-up Parisienne has a
chic Petit Bateau T-shirt, a brand
known for its excellent quality and
fit. The company is also renowned
for its well-made everyday baby
and children's collections.

🔲 b2 ✉ 50 rue des Abbesses, 75018
☎ 01 42 52 81 76 🕒 Mon–Sat 10–7
🚇 Abbesses

PIERRE HERMÉ
pierreherme.com

The couture pastries are as
visually stunning as they are
mouthwatering and the gold-leaf
ornamented chocolate cake is
legendary. Or take home a delight-
fully presented box of *macarons*
(macaroons) as a gift.

🔲 G7 ✉ 72 rue Bonaparte, 75006
☎ 01 43 54 47 77 🕒 Daily 10–7
🚇 Saint-Sulpice, Mabillon

RUE MOUFFETARD

Visit this tourist classic straggling
down a narrow, hilly street, for a
wonderful array of shops and stalls
selling fruit and veg, *charcuterie*
and aromatic cheeses. There are
good café stops en route.

🔲 J9 ✉ Rue Mouffetard, 75005 🕒 Daily,
but some shops and stalls close Sun–Mon
🚇 Monge

LE SEPT CINQ
sept-cinq.com

For stylish clothing or jewelry by
local creatives, head to this
concept store. Everything on sale
is by Parisian designers, including
socks by Royalties and espadrilles
by Barre Paris.

🔲 B3 ✉ 54 rue Notre-Dame-de-Lorette,
75009 ☎ 09 83 55 05 95 🕒 Mon–Sat
11.30–7.30 🚇 Pigalle

SHAKESPEARE AND COMPANY
shakespeareandcompany.com

Opened in 1951, this English language bookstore quickly became a magnet for ex-pat writers and wannabe literary characters. Allen Ginsberg and Henry Miller were just two of the literary giants who came here.

➕ J7 ✉ 37 rue de la Bûcherie, 75005
☎ 01 43 25 40 93 🕐 Daily 10am–11pm
🚇 Saint-Michel

SI TU VEUX
situveuxjouer.com

The perfect toy shop, Si Tu Veux sells affordable toys, games and dressing-up clothes and other accessories. There's a good range of options for creative play for all ages, excellent old-style wooden toys and a separate section devoted to teddy bears.

➕ H4 ✉ 68 Galerie Vivienne, 75002
☎ 01 42 60 59 97 🕐 Mon–Sat 10.30–7
🚇 Bourse

SONIA RYKIEL
soniarykiel.com

In business since 1968, this classic ready-to-wear fashion house was founded by Paris-born Sonia (1930–2016) and is now run by her daughter Nathalie. It also sells ranges of accessories and perfumes and has launched youth and children's lines.

➕ G6 ✉ 175 boulevard Saint-Germain, 75006 ☎ 01 49 54 60 60 🕐 Mon–Sat 10.30–7 🚇 Saint-Germain-des-Prés

STOHRER
stohrer.fr

When the Polish wife of King Louis XV moved into Versailles palace she brought her *patissier*, Nicolas Stohrer, with her. Five years later he opened this shop and here, it is said, the delectable rum baba was invented.

➕ J4 ✉ 51 rue Montorgueil, 75002
☎ 01 40 33 38 20 🕐 Daily 7.30–8.30
🚇 Les Halles

VANESSA BRUNO
vanessabruno.com

This designer's practical, easy-to-wear women's clothing has won her a loyal following. The 1960s and '70s inspired designs are renowned for their stylish flair. The recently launched "cabas" leather bag has become a classic must-have item.

➕ L5 ✉ 100 rue Vieille-du-Temple, 75003
☎ 01 42 77 19 41 🕐 Mon 12.30–7.30,
Tue–Sat 10.30–7.30, Sun 2–7 🚇 Filles du Calvaire

ZADIG & VOLTAIRE
zadig-et-voltaire.com

There's a youthful edge to the men's and womenswear at this Left Bank outpost of the internationally successful fashion house founded by Frenchman Thierry Gillier, son of the founder of the Lacoste empire.

➕ G6 ✉ 200 boulevard Saint-Germain, 75005 ☎ 01 45 49 10 34 🕐 Mon–Sat 10.30–7.30 🚇 Saint-Germain-des-Prés

BOUTIQUING

The streets around the Abbesses Métro station offer a treasure trove of quirky independent clothing, accessories and gift boutiques. For fabulous food shops head down the rue des Abbesses and turn left on rue Lepic. Another wonderful food shopping area in Montmartre is the stretch of rue des Martyrs that descends below the boulevard de Clichy.

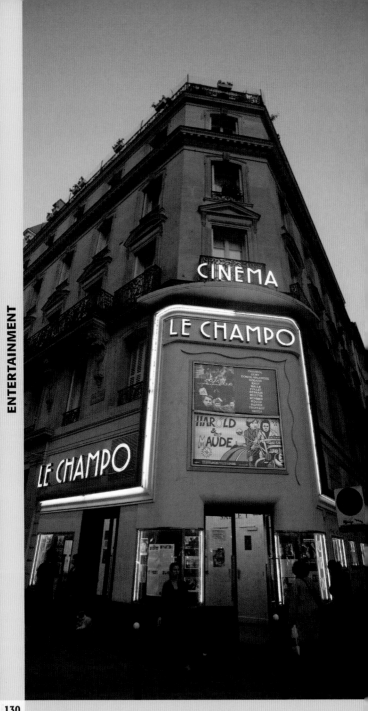

Entertainment

Once you've done with sightseeing for the day, you'll find lots of other great things to do with your time in this chapter, even if all you want to do is relax with a drink. In this section establishments are listed alphabetically.

ENTERTAINMENT

Introduction

The heart of Paris has a special beauty at night, and an electric atmosphere. Boulevards, great monuments and historic buildings are dazzlingly illuminated. The Champs-Élysées, place de la Concorde and the Louvre make a magnificent spectacle of lights against the night sky. The soaring Eiffel Tower, shining like gold and glittering for five minutes every hour, and the silvery white of the Sacré-Cœur Basilica are majestic landmarks.

Nightlife by Area

In a city as big as Paris there is no single focus for nightlife, and where you go will depend on what you are looking for. Small theaters and jazz clubs still dot the Left Bank, and there are more jazz clubs around Châtelet and Les Halles. While there's a chic and expensive feel to many of the bars and clubs in the west, between Étoile and Opéra, Montmartre, Pigalle and Clichy offer nightlife of an altogether more raffish kind. However, their many sex shops and strip joints are interspersed with mainstream discos and some of the city's best live music venues, so that it's not an area to be written off as too sleazy. The eastern *arrondissements* have some of the most interesting and fashionable nightlife, from the Marais's GLBTQ scene and

AN EVENING STROLL

Start at Châtelet and walk toward the Louvre along the embankment opposite the illuminated Conciergerie, the Monnaie and the Institut de France. At the Louvre make a detour into the magnificently lit Cour Carrée. Return to the river, cross the Pont des Arts, then walk back along the opposite bank, with views north to the stately Samaritaine and the Palais de Justice on the Île de la Cité. Continue toward Saint-Michel, then cross over to Notre-Dame and make your way around the north side of the island for good views.

Clockwise from top: Evening view of the domed Institut de France, with the Pont des Arts in the foreground; the Opera Bastille; cafés, bars and clubs line the streets of

branché (trendy) café society to the scuffed boho chic of lively rue Oberkampf.

Glamorous Fun
There's a sense of excitement, anticipation and enjoyment in Paris. In addition to glamorous cabarets, there are world-class ballet, concert and opera venues, nightclubs, discos, café-theaters and atmospheric bars with live music. Although the Métro is closed from 1.15am (2.15 Friday and Saturday) to 5.30am, plenty of taxis run at night, as well as the Noctilien buses (ratp.fr).

Clubbing Paris Style
Dressing up—not down—is still often the rule when you go dancing in Paris, and if your clothes don't pass muster you may not get past the door at some clubs. Drinks prices can be steep but the price of entry often includes a *conso* (free drink).

Added Magic
A boat trip along the Seine between the illuminated buildings adds extra magic, and *bateaux mouches* run every evening until 10.30 (9.20 in winter). For experienced in-line skaters a high-speed three-hour skating tour of Paris takes place every Friday at 9.30pm (see pari-roller.com for details).

GLBTQ PARIS

As befits a 21st-century, cosmopolitan city that had an openly gay mayor—Bertrand Delanoë—from 2001 to 2014, Paris is a welcoming place for GLBTQ visitors, particularly in the fashionable Marais district, where the list of entertainment venues stretches beyond the established confines of the official scene. The hugely popular Open Café (✉ 17 rue des Archives ☎ 01 42 72 26 18, opencafe.fr) and slick Raidd (✉ 23 rue du Temple; raiddbar.com) are two of the area's best places to see and be seen in.

Montmartre; enjoying a night out; a delightful evening scene in Paris; there are plenty of clubs to choose from; the famous Moulin Rouge

Directory

Entertainment A–Z

AUDITORIUM DU LOUVRE

louvre.fr

A high-quality series of lunchtime and evening concerts are held in this 450-seat auditorium beneath the Louvre's pyramid. Currently Wednesday evenings offers chamber music, while Thursday afternoons are dedicated to rising talent, and Friday evenings to popular classics and music commissioned by the museum.

🟦 G5 ✉ Musée du Louvre (entrance by the pyramid), 75001 ☎ 01 40 20 55 55 Ⓜ Palais-Royal

LE BALZAC

cinemabalzac.com

Le Balzac is famous for its screenings of American independent films (in the original language) and for the debates that often follow. Concerts are held before Saturday evening screenings. Bar on site.

🟦 B3 ✉ 1 rue Balzac, 75008 ☎ 01 45 61 10 60 Ⓜ George V, Charles de Gaulle–Étoile

LE BAR DU BRISTOL

lebristolparis.com

Set in the high-class Le Bristol hotel, this equally elegant bar is one of the top cocktail venues in the city, whose inventive mixologist has created a menu of classic and new drinks. There are DJ sessions Tuesday to Saturday.

🟦 E3 ✉ 112 rue du Faubourg Saint-Honoré, 75008 ☎ 01 53 43 43 00 🕐 Daily 5.30pm–2am Ⓜ Miromesnil

BARRAMUNDI

barramundi.fr

Barramundi draws a fashionable crowd with its world music, bar, lounge and eclectic restaurant. This is one of Paris's top chill-out spots.

🟦 H3 ✉ 3 rue Taitbout, 75009 ☎ 01 47

70 21 21 🕐 Mon–Fri 12–3.30pm, 6.30pm–2am, Sat 7pm–5am Ⓜ Richelieu–Drouot, Chaussée d'Antin

LA BOULE NOIRE/LA CIGALE

lacigale.fr

Famous names have played at the diminutive La Boule Noire, including Franz Ferdinand, Jamie Cullum and Metallica. It's linked to a former theater, La Cigale, a listed historic monument, and hosts musicals, rock and pop, and music festivals.

🟦 c2 ✉ 120 boulevard Rochechouart, 75018 ☎ 01 49 25 89 99 Ⓜ Pigalle, Anvers

CAVEAU DE LA HUCHETTE

caveaudelahuchette.fr

Still going strong after 60 years, having hosted many of the great names in jazz, this basement bar hosts live jazz and dancing.

🟦 J7 ✉ 5 rue de la Huchette, 75005 ☎ 01 43 26 65 05 🕐 Daily from 9.30pm Ⓜ Saint-Michel

LE CHAMPO

lechampo.com

Come here for cult classics, with retrospectives of famous directors such as the Marx Brothers, Claude Chabrol and Jacques Tati. Films are in the original language.

CONCERTS

Numerous classical music concerts are held in churches—try Saint-Eustache, Saint-Germain-des-Prés, Saint-Julien-le-Pauvre, Saint-Louis-en-l'Île, Saint-Roch and Saint-Séverin (ampconcerts.com). Seats are reasonably priced and the quality of music is sometimes very high. From May to September free concerts are held in parks. Schedules are available at the Office du Tourisme or the Hôtel de Ville.

🗺 J7 ✉ 51 rue des Écoles, 75015 ☎ 01 43 54 51 60 🕐 Daily, times vary 🚇 Saint-Michel, Odéon, Cluny–La Sorbonne

LE CLUB
the-club.fr
Renowned mixologists Seb and Olivier create some of Paris's best cocktails at their bar designed by stylist Philippe Modal. There's a long cocktail menu, and they'll be happy to oblige if you request something unique.
🗺 D5 ✉ 24 Rue Surcouf, 75007 ☎ 01 45 50 31 54 🕐 Mon–Sat 4pm–2am 🚇 Invalides

CLUB L'ARC
larc-paris.com
This long-standing favorite has been renovated by American rock star Lenny Kravitz. It's now one of the most fashionable places in town.
🗺 B2 ✉ 12 rue de Presbourg, 75016 ☎ 0659 21 32 44 🕐 Thu from 10 for women, midnight for men; Fri–Sat from midnight for both sexes 🚇 Charles de Gaulle–Étoile

COMÉDIE FRANÇAISE/ SALLE RICHELIEU
comedie-francaise.fr
The Comédie Française, home to France's most prestigious troupe of actors, was founded by Louis XIV in 1680. Today, the repertoire is made up of the classics, including works by Shakespeare, Molière and Victor Hugo, and a few modern pieces.
🗺 G4 ✉ 1 place Colette, 75001 ☎ 01 44 58 15 15 🕐 Performances daily, times vary, some matinées Sat, Sun 🚇 Palais-Royal–Musée du Louvre

COMPAGNIE DES VINS SURNATURELS
compagniedesvinssurnaturels.com
Enjoy some of France's finest wines by the glass in this elegant lounge. Parisians arrive here after work for pre-dinner drinks or come later in the evening to savor some of the country's most prestigious labels.
🗺 H7 ✉ 7 rue Lobineau, 75006 ☎ 09 54 90 20 20 🕐 Daily 6pm–2am 🚇 Mabillon

CONCRETE
concreteparis.fr
At the forefront in the resurgence of after-hours and all-day dance clubs, this large space plays host to the latest sounds and DJ sets.
🗺 M9 ✉ Port de la Rapée, 75012 ☎ 0628 52 00 18 🕐 Fri 9pm–7am, Sat 9pm–7am, Sun 7am–2am 🚇 Quai de la Gare

LE CRAZY HORSE
lecrazyhorseparis.com
This world-renowned burlesque show has been wowing audiences with its naughty but humorous routines, gorgeous dancers and dazzling, albeit scanty, costumes by top designers since 1951.

C4 12 avenue George V, 75008
01 47 23 32 32 Shows: Sun–Fri
8.15 and 10.45, Sat 7, 9.30 and 11.45
George V, Alma–Marceau

DELAVILLE
delavilleparis.com

Opened in the 1860s, Delaville
embraces the zeitgeist by trans-
forming itself from café and tea
bar by day into club and cabaret
as night falls. It has a vibe that
harks back to the Josephine Baker
era with DJ sets and dancers.
J3 34–36 Boulevard Bonne Nouvelle,
75010 01 48 24 48 09 Daily
8.30am–2am Bonne Nouvelle

DIVAN DU MONDE
divandumonde.com

Devoted to French music, this
former brothel and club is now
one of the latest Francophone
venues. The regular program
ranges from live cabaret with
Madame Arthur to French dance
and club music sessions.
C3 75 rue des Martyrs, 75018
01 40 05 08 10 Wed–Sat 8pm–6am
Pigalle

DUC DES LOMBARDS
ducdeslombards.com

Prestigious jazz musicians regularly
play in this Les Halles club. Late
night Friday and Saturday there's
free entry for a free-form jam
session that carries on until the
early hours.
J5 42 rue des Lombards, 75001
01 42 33 22 88 Closed Sun
Châtelet

FAVELA CHIC
favelachic.com

The sounds, flavors and vibrant
style of urban Brazil pound out in
this club, with a restaurant, live
bands and DJs. It includes a
pop-up gallery and a quirky,
chill-out lounge zone.
M3 18 rue du Faubourg du Temple,
75011 01 40 21 31 14 Tue–Sat
7.30pm–late Pigalle

FORUM DES IMAGES
forumdesimages.fr

Films or documentaries shot in or
connected with Paris and movie
classics are screened here, along
with independent documentaries
from around the world. A day pass
admits you to all screenings. Visit
the website for other venues
around the city.
J5 2 rue du Cinéma, Port Saint-
Eustache, Forum des Halles, 75001 01
44 76 63 00 Tue–Fri 12.30pm–9pm,
Sat–Sun 2pm–9pm Les Halles, Châtelet

HARRY'S NEW YORK BAR
harrysbar.fr

Harry's in New York was dismantled and shipped lock, stock and
barrel to Paris just before World
War I. It's famous for having
hundreds of cocktails.
G3 5 rue Daunou, 75002 01 42
61 71 14 Mon–Sat 12noon–2am, Sun
4pm–1am Opéra

POOLS AND HORSES

Paris's municipal swimming pools have
complicated opening hours largely geared
to schoolchildren. Phone to check for
public hours and avoid Wednesday and
Saturday, popular times for children off
school. If horse-racing is your passion,
don't miss the harness-racing at Vincennes
(letrot.com), with its brilliant flashes of
color-coordinated horses and jockeys.
Check the racing newspaper *Paris-Turf*
(paris-turf.com) for race schedules.

LUCERNAIRE/CENTRE NATIONAL D'ART ET D'ESSAI

lucernaire.fr

This complex of three cinemas, an art gallery, bar, restaurant and three theaters stages a wide variety of plays. Housed in a former factory, it attracts top French actors.

➕ G8 ✉ 53 rue Notre-Dame-des-Champs, 75006 ☎ 01 45 44 57 34 🚇 Vavin, Notre-Dame-des-Champs

MICHOU

michou.com

A familiar sight in the district, Michou is always dressed in electric-blue suits and big eye-glasses. The drag show in this venerable club is still going strong.

➕ c2 ✉ 80 rue des Martyrs, 75018 ☎ 01 46 06 16 04 🕙 Nightly dinner 8.30pm, show 10.30pm 🚇 Pigalle

MOULIN ROUGE

moulinrouge.fr

The Red Windmill, made famous by Toulouse-Lautrec, opened in 1889 when audiences flocked to ogle at the dancers performing the cancan. These days the shows are still as spectacular but are more entertaining than scandalous.

➕ b2 ✉ 82 boulevard de Clichy, 75018 ☎ 01 53 09 82 82 🕙 Nightly dinner

BEAUTIFUL PEOPLE

The clubs around the Champs-Élysées tend to attract VIPs, celebrities and a generally well-heeled crowd. Clubs usually don't open until 11pm or midnight, and often stay open until dawn. For a more laid-back, arty bar scene, go to the bar-lined rue Oberkampf or the Canal Saint-Martin area. The Marais district is also packed with bars, many of them gay or mixed.

and show 7pm; show only 9 and 11pm; see website for matinee performances 🚇 Blanche

MUSÉE DE CLUNY – MUSÉE-NATIONAL DU MOYEN-ÂGE

musee-moyenage.fr

This medieval mansion is home to a museum devoted to the Middle Ages (▷ 30–31), but it also hosts classical and chamber music concerts. Most appropriate are the concerts of medieval music in conjunction with the Centre de musique médiévale de Paris.

➕ J7 ✉ 6 place Paul-Painlevé, 75005 ☎ 01 53 73 78 16 🕙 Free concerts of medieval music: times vary 🚇 Cluny–La Sorbonne

OPÉRA BASTILLE

operadeparis.fr

Paris's opera house towers over place de la Bastille and boasts five movable stages. Performances include opera, operettas, recitals, ballet, dance and theater.

➕ M7 ✉ 130 rue de Lyon, 75012 ☎ 08 92 89 90 90 🚇 Bastille

PHILHARMONIE DE PARIS

philharmoniedeparis.fr

Inaugurated in 2015, the city's new, 1,500-seat venue, is home to the Orchestre de Paris and offers a rich program of solo artists, classical and rock concerts, family events and music workshops.

➕ Off map at M1 ✉ 221 avenue Jean Jaurès, Parc de la Villette, 75019 ☎ 01 44 84 44 84 🚇 Porte de Pintin

QUEEN

queen.fr

This large club is still going strong and is popular with both straight and gay people. It hosts many top

DJs, with different themes each evening. The doormen are known to be very particular, so make sure you dress well.

➕ C3 ✉ 79 avenue des Champs-Élysées, 75008 ☎ 01 53 89 08 90 🕐 Daily midnight–7am (times can vary, some nights start earlier) 🚇 George V

STUDIO 28

cinema-studio28.com

Studio 28 is a stylish cinema in Paris, where new releases in the original language change every day or two, and French classics are screened every month. It has its own little bar and garden where you can mingle with like-minded film aficionados.

➕ b2 ✉ 10 rue Tholozé, 75018 ☎ 01 46 06 36 07 🕐 Daily 3–9pm (start of last showing) 🚇 Abbesses, Blanche

STUDIO GALANDE

studiogalande.fr

Cult movie *The Rocky Horror Picture Show* is shown here every Friday and Saturday at 10pm. The rest of the week screenings range from art films to cartoons.

➕ J7 ✉ 42 rue Galande, 75005 ☎ 01 43 54 72 71 🕐 Screenings daily from noon 🚇 Saint-Michel, Maubert–Mutualité, Cluny

SUNSET-SUNSIDE

sunset-sunside.com

Opened in 1984 as a venue for jazz of all descriptions, this club has evolved over the years into two jazz clubs: the Sunset offers a range of electric jazz and world music concerts, while the Sunside concentrates on acoustic jazz.

➕ J5 ✉ 60 rue des Lombards, 75001 ☎ 01 40 26 46 60 🕐 Live performances daily 8.30pm or 9pm 🚇 Châtelet

---

PARIS'S MEGA VENUES

Stade de France (stadedefrance.com), seating 80,000, is France's biggest stadium and hosts national sports games in addition to rock bands. AccorHotelsArena (accorhotelsarena.com), in Bercy to the southeast, is a 20,000-capacity venue. Finally, the city's newest mega-venue, the futuristic Philharmonie de Paris (▷ 138), hosts classical and contemporary acts.

THÉÂTRE DU CHÂTELET

chatelet-theatre.com

The Théâtre du Châtelet hosts a varied schedule of opera, symphonic music and dance, as well as popular Sunday morning concerts. It seats 2,500 people.

➕ J6 ✉ 2 rue Edouard Colonne, 75001 ☎ 01 40 28 28 28 🕐 Check website calender 🚇 Châtelet

THÉÂTRE DE LA HUCHETTE

theatre-huchette.com

Two of Ionesco's masterpieces, *La Cantatrice Chauve* (The Bald Soprano) and *La Leçon* (The Lesson), have been performed here five days a week for over 50 years. It's an intimate venue with room for just 85 people.

➕ J7 ✉ 23 rue de la Huchette, 75005 ☎ 01 43 26 38 99 🕐 Tue–Sat 7pm and 8pm 🚇 Saint-Michel

THÉÂTRE DE LA VILLE

theatredelaville-paris.com

This modern venue showcases an adventurous program of avant-garde music, classical pieces, contemporary dance and plays, which include well-directed works by Shakespeare and Marlowe.

➕ J6 ✉ 1 avenue Gabriel, 75004 ☎ 01 42 74 22 77 🕐 Performance times vary 🚇 Châtelet

Eat

There are places to eat across the city to suit all tastes and budgets. In this section establishments are listed alphabetically.

EAT

Introduction

Paris is often described as the capital of gastronomy, so a meal out in the city has a lot to live up to. The standard for the best restaurants—the Michelin star—is famed throughout the world as the epitome of gastronomic excellence.

Budget Choices
If your budget isn't up to the crème-de-la-crème, there are hundreds of less expensive choices, from regional French cuisine to North African, Lebanese or Japanese.

The Very Best
Restaurants have higher prices than brasseries or bistros but will often provide a refined setting, elegant cuisine and a good wine list. For a special treat, look for multistarred Michelin chefs such as Alain Ducasse and Guy Savoy. Dress smartly and book in advance.

Lunch and Snacks
Cafés and bars serve coffee, tea, soft drinks, alcohol and snacks. Most open from around 9am (or earlier) until well into the evening and many have outdoor seating. *Salons de thé* (tearooms) open from noon until evening. If you are on a budget, have your main meal at lunchtime, when most restaurants serve a reasonably priced *menu du jour*, or daily menu, of two or three courses with a glass of wine.

OPENING TIMES

Most restaurants and bistros keep strict serving times. Restaurants open at 12, close at 2.30, then reopen at 7.30 or 8. Most Parisians take an hour for lunch and eat in the staff canteen or in a local bistro. The evening meal is the most important of the day and is usually taken *en famille* between 8 and 9pm. Restaurants stop taking orders between 10 and 11pm. To eat later, try the Les Halles area or a brasserie. Some places close on weekends and in July and August, and for holidays in February.

From top: A table with a view at Le Jules Verne restaurant, Tour Eiffel; stopping for coffee; blackboard menu; a colorful dish at Guy Savoy's restaurant

EAT

Directory

AROUND THE TOUR EIFFEL
Asian
Benkay
French-Bistro
L'Affriolé
Bistrotrotters
French-Brasserie
Brasserie Thoumieux
French-Elegant
Le Jules Verne
French-Regional
L'Ami Jean

LATIN QUARTER, ST-GERMAIN AND ISLANDS
Asian
Desi Road
French-Bistro
Café St. Regis
Le Comptoir
Les Papilles
Le Petit Saint-Benoît
Ze Kitchen Galerie
French-Brasserie
Alcazar
La Coupole
French-Elegant
Guy Savoy
La Tour d'Argent
La Truffière

MARAIS AND BASTILLE
French-Bistro
L'Ange 20
Au Pied de Cochon
Bistrot Paul Bert
Chez Paul
Monjul
Pramil
Restaurant Frenchie
French-Brasserie
Bofinger

French-Regional
Benoit
Kosher
L'As du Fallafel
North African
404

LOUVRE AND CHAMPS-ÉLYSÉES
Café/Creperie
Midi 12
French-Bistro
L'Avenue
Café Marly
French-Elegant
Le Céladon
Epicure
Passage 53
Taillevent
French-Regional
Carré des Feuillants
Fusion
6 New York

MONTMARTRE
French-Bistro
Au Virage Lepic
Le Progrès
Seb'on
French-Regional
Au Clair de la Lune
Italian/Mediterranean
Pink Mamma
Organic
Rose Bakery

FARTHER AFIELD
French-Bistro
La Petite Ardoise
Septime
French-Elegant
Gordon Ramsay au Trianon

EAT

Eating A–Z

Prices are approximate, based on a three-course meal for one person.

€€€	over €90
€€	€35–€90
€	under €35

6 NEW YORK €€

6newyork.fr

For beautiful contemporary decor and fusion food, head for 6 New York. Chef and owner Jerome Gangneux, who hails from Normandy, cooks with a lightness of touch that allows the fresh ingredients to reveal their flavors.

🚹 B5 ✉ 6 avenue de New York, 75016 ☎ 01 40 70 03 30 🕐 Mon–Fri lunch, dinner, Sat dinner 🚇 Alma–Marceau

404 €–€€

404-resto.com

This family-run restaurant serves excellent North African cuisine. Beautifully styled, it's like stepping into an Arab souk, with colorful ceramics, fine basketry and carpets festooning the walls. The dining room is part of an atmospheric 16th-century building.

🚹 K4 ✉ 69 rue des Gravilliers, 75003 ☎ 01 42 74 57 81 🕐 Daily lunch, dinner 🚇 Arts et Métiers

L'AFFRIOLÉ €€

laffriole.fr

This great value nouveau bistro provides friendly service and classic French dishes. All wines are available by the glass, which is rare in Paris.

🚹 C5 ✉ 17 rue Malar, 75007 ☎ 01 85 15 23 93 🕐 Tue–Sat lunch, dinner 🚇 La Tour Maubourg, Pont de l'Alma, Invalides

ALCAZAR €€

alcazar.fr

One of the city's first modern bistros, Alcazar remains a city favorite after a total renovation. Michel Besmond oversees a selection of freshly prepared adventurous dishes, served in the eclectically styled yet relaxed dining room.

🚹 H6 ✉ 62 rue Mazarine, 75006 ☎ 01 53 10 19 99 🕐 Daily lunch, dinner 🚇 Odéon

Coffees and beers in the Marais district

L'AMI JEAN €€

lamijean.fr

Owned by chef Stéphane Jego, an apprentice of pioneer Yves Camdeborde, this friendly restaurant serves traditional Basque dishes of beef and seafood with a contemporary slant and enhanced by fine wines.

🚇 C5 ✉ 27 rue Malar, 75007 ☎ 01 47 05 86 89 🕐 Tue–Sat lunch, dinner 🚇 Pont de l'Alma, La Tour Maubourg, Invalides

L'ANGE 20 €€

lange20.com

The team keep their menu very simple with each course (a choice of two or three dishes) at a set price. The menu features fresh French ingredients served with a modern twist and elegantly executed.

🚇 K5 ✉ 44 rue des Tournelles, 75004 ☎ 01 85 15 23 92 🕐 Wed–Sun lunch, dinner 🚇 Bastille

L'AS DU FALLAFEL €

This kosher restaurant has a cult following among visitors and Marais locals alike for its falafel and low prices. You'll probably have to wait in line, but it will be worth it. There is also a take out menu.

🚇 L6 ✉ 34 rue des Rosiers, 75007 ☎ 01 48 87 63 60 🕐 Sun–Thu 12–12, Fri lunch only 🚇 Saint-Paul

AU CLAIR DE LA LUNE €€

clairedelalune.fr

Classic French cuisine is served in this comfortable, welcoming inn-style restaurant just off the place du Tertre. It is run by two brothers and is popular with locals.

🚇 C1 ✉ 9 rue Poulbot, 75018 ☎ 01 42 58 97 03 🕐 Daily lunch, dinner 🚇 Abbesses

AU PIED DE COCHON €€

pieddecochon.com

Pigs' trotters feature at this Parisian institution, along with seafood and sublime French onion soup, served in elegant surroundings. It attracts Parisians and tourists alike and is extremely popular with the late-night set.

🚇 J4 ✉ 6 rue Coquillère, 75001 ☎ 01 40 13 77 00 🕐 Daily 24 hours 🚇 Les Halles

AU VIRAGE LEPIC €–€€

This welcoming bistro is well known for its tasty meat-based main courses and delicious puddings, complemented by a great wine list. In summer, you can sit outside.

🚇 b1 ✉ 61 rue Lepic, 75018 ☎ 01 42 52 46 79 🕐 Wed–Mon dinner 🚇 Blanche, Abbesses

L'AVENUE €€

avenue-restaurant.com

The terrace of this long-standing café is perfect for people watching in one of the cities most upmarket districts. The menu features typical bistro fare.

🚇 C4 ✉ 41 avenue Montaigne, 75008 ☎ 01 40 70 14 91 🕐 Daily 8am–2am 🚇 Franklin D Roosevelt

BENKAY €€

restaurant-benkay.com

Dine here on modern Japanese food and enjoy the panoramic views from the fourth floor of the Novotel Paris Tour Eiffel. Choose from a full-service sushi bar, a *washoku* traditional Japanese menu, and a showy *teppanyaki* station.

🚇 A7 ✉ 61 quai de Grenelle, 75015 ☎ 01 40 58 21 26 🕐 Daily lunch, dinner 🚇 Bir-Hakeim

EAT

It is said that Cathérine de Médici, the Italian wife of Henri II, invented French cuisine in the 16th century—though Gallic opinions may differ. Italian food is very popular in Paris. In addition to the pizza-and-pasta establishments, there are many fine restaurants specializing in the most sophisticated Italian cuisine.

BENOIT €€–€€€
benoit-paris.com

This long-standing bistro serving classic regional dishes is owned by renowned chef Alain Ducasse. The dining room has an elegant period interior, matched by the food that is served by knowledgeable staff. Reserve ahead.

J6 ⊠ 20 rue Saint-Martin, 75004 ☎ 01 58 00 22 05 🕐 Daily lunch, dinner Ⓜ Hôtel de Ville, Châtelet-Les Halles

BISTROT PAUL BERT €€

One of the last old-style bistros, Bistrot Paul Bert has a loyal clien-tele that comes back for its generous portions, the best steak in town, and a cheese plate that takes you on a dairy tour of France.

Off map ⊠ 18 rue Paul Bert 75011 🕐 01 43 72 24 01 🕐 Tue–Sat lunch, dinner Ⓜ Faidherbe–Chaligny,

BISTROTTERS €€
bistrotters.com

A small culinary team brings the flavors of the world to French ingredients in a menu that changes with the seasons. There's a wine shop on site where you can stock up on the bottles you enjoyed over dinner.

Off map ⊠ 9 rue Decrès, 75014 ☎ 01 45 45 58 59 🕐 Daily lunch, dinner Ⓜ Plaisance

BOFINGER €€
bofingerparis.com

Claiming to be the oldest brasserie in Paris (1864), Bofinger adheres strongly to the traditional brasserie menu and serves seafood, *choucroute* and steaks, plus the ubiquitous onion soup. The refined interior is period-perfect art nouveau in style.

M6 ⊠ 5 rue de la Bastille, 75004 ☎ 01 42 72 87 82 🕐 Daily lunch, dinner Ⓜ Bastille

BRASSERIE THOUMIEUX €€
thoumieux.com

Established in 1923, Thoumieux's mirrored walls and red velvet seats hark back to a classic era. Expect hearty *cassoulet* (sausage and bean casserole) and duck dishes. Upstairs is the pricey fine-dining Restaurant Sylvestre.

D5 ⊠ 79 rue Saint-Dominique, 75007 ☎ 01 47 05 79 00 🕐 Daily lunch, dinner Ⓜ Invalides

CAFÉ MARLY €€
cafe-marly.com

This café-restaurant in the Louvre must have one of the best terraces in the world, with its exceptional view of architect I.M. Pei's stunning glass pyramid framing the opposite wing of the museum. The food on offer here is good and the service is friendly.

G5 ⊠ 93 rue de Rivoli, 75001 ☎ 01 49 26 06 60 🕐 Daily 8am–2am (last orders midnight) Ⓜ Palais-Royal–Musée du Louvre

CAFÉ ST. REGIS €–€€
cafesaintregisparis.com

The menu of this traditional French café melds Gallic classics with contemporary fashion, with

The French are famous for their crusty bread

croque monsieur sitting side by side with tapas sardines. Enjoy the atmosphere of Île Saint-Louis from the terrace on a balmy summer evening.

🔸 K7 ✉ rue Jean du Bellay, Île Saint-Louis, 75004 ☎ 01 43 54 59 41 🕐 Daily 6am–2am 🚇 Pont Marie, Sully Morland

CARRÉ DES FEUILLANTS €€€

carredesfeuillants.fr

You'll find an elegant setting for Alain Dutournier's evocation of the cooking of his native Gascony. He uses the best ingredients to wonderful effect, earning a high reputation for his restaurant.

🔸 F4 ✉ 14 rue de Castiglione, 75001 ☎ 01 42 86 82 82 🕐 Mon–Fri lunch, dinner. Closed Aug 🚇 Tuileries

LE CÉLADON €€–€€€

leceladon.com

Serving interesting variations on French classics, Le Céladon offers a good-value weekday lunch menu that is ideal for anyone wanting to explore French haute-cuisine. It opens as Le Petit Céladon on weekends.

🔸 G3 ✉ Hotel Westminster, 15 rue Daunou, 75002 ☎ 01 47 03 40 42 🕐 Mon–Fri lunch, dinner. Closed Aug 🚇 Opéra

CHEZ PAUL €–€€

chezpaul.com

One of the last authentic Paris bistros serves staples such as snails and onion soup at very reasonable prices. Just like the menu, the decor hasn't been changed in decades, which makes it all the more fun.

🔸 Off map ✉ 13 rue de Charonne 75011 ☎ 01 47 00 34 57 🕐 Daily lunch, dinner 🚇 Bastille, Ledru Rollin

LE COMPTOIR €€

hotel-paris-relais-saint-germain.com

At the vanguard of the movement, this gastro-bistro, under the expert eye of chef Yves Camdeborde, champions modern French cuisine. Reservations are not taken for lunch, but it's best to reserve ahead for dinner.

🔸 H7 ✉ Hôtel Relais Saint-Germain, 9 carrefour de l'Odéon, 75006 ☎ 01 44 27 07 97 🕐 Daily lunch, dinner 🚇 Odéon

LA COUPOLE €€

lacoupole-paris.com

This Montparnasse brasserie offers reasonably priced set menus plus all the standard dishes, but the elegant art deco setting and buzzy ambience are what make this place memorable.

✉ 102 boulevard du Montparnasse, 75014 ☎ 01 43 20 14 20 🕐 Daily lunch, dinner 🚇 Vavin

DESI ROAD €€

desiroadrestaurant.com

One of the city's best Indian restaurants, with beautiful decor and attentive service, Desi Road serves a range of traditional curries.
H6 ✉ 14 rue Dauphine, 75006 ☎ 01 85 15 26 90 🕐 Tue–Sun lunch, dinner 🚇 Pont Neuf, Odéon

EPICURE €€€

lebristolparis.com

Eric Frechon's superb restaurant offers the epitome of French gastronomic dining within the magnificent Bristol Hotel. Expect an inventive menu to titillate the taste buds. The hotel's attractive gardens make a wonderful place for an alfresco dinner during the summer.
D3 ✉ 112 rue du Faubourg Saint Honoré, 75008 ☎ 01 53 43 43 00 🕐 Daily breakfast, lunch, dinner 🚇 Saint-Philippe du Roule

GORDON RAMSAY AU TRIANON €€€

gordonramsay.com

Round off a day of splendor in spectacular Versailles with a sumptuous dinner in Gordon Ramsay's much-praised dining room in the Trianon Palace Hotel, where the menu makes lavish use of luxurious ingredients such as lobster and foie gras. Reservations are recommended.
Off map ✉ 1 boulevard de la Reine, 78000, Versailles ☎ 01 30 84 50 18 🕐 Tue–Sat dinner 🚉 SNCF Versailles Rive Droite or RER Versailles Rive Gauche

GUY SAVOY €€€

guysavoy.com

At this gastronomic temple, in a stunning new home at La Monnaie de Paris (Paris Mint building), chef Guy Savoy turns cooking into an art form. It is expensive to dine here, of course, but it is also exquisite; expect an unforgettable dining experience.
H6 ✉ Monnaie de Paris, 11 quai de Conti, 75006 ☎ 01 43 80 40 61 🕐 Tue–Fri lunch, dinner, Sat dinner 🚇 Pont Neuf

Delectable oysters

NEW BISTROS

Paris may be the food capital of the world, with more than its share of top restaurants, but not everyone can afford the astronomical prices of the best eateries. Some 15 years ago a few famous chefs rebelled against this situation and opened "baby bistros," which offered fine meals in often nondescript surroundings for reasonable prices. The trend has now expanded and Paris is full of nouveaux bistros.

LE JULES VERNE €€€

lejulesverne-paris.com

Alain Ducasse's wonderful restaurant can be found 125 metres above the streets of Paris on level two of the Eiffel Tower. Since it opened its doors in 2007, Le Jules Verne has been the talk of the city with its superb food and fabulous panoramic day and nighttime views. Reservations are essential here.

🗺 B6 ✉ 2nd level, Tour Eiffel, 75007 (private elevator) ☎ 01 45 55 61 44 🕐 Daily lunch, dinner Ⓜ Bir-Hakeim

MIDI 12 €

midi12.com

This tiny, bright modern cafe serves beautifully presented sweet and savory crêpes throughout the afternoon, which makes it an excellent pit stop for a quick yet filling lunch after a morning shopping on Boulevard Haussmann. It's a good option for vegans and vegetarians.

🗺 G2 ✉ 12 Rue la Fayette, 75009 ☎ 09 50 12 24 24 🕐 Mon–Fri 12 noon–5.30pm, Sat 8.30–10am, 12 noon–5.30pm Ⓜ Chausée d'Antin La Fayette

MONJUL €€

monjul.com

At Monjul, the talented Julien Agobert, one of an exciting new generation of daring and experimental chefs, produces exciting and inventive dishes that are works of art—and taste just as good, if not better, than they look. There's liberal use of pretty, edible flowers that give the dishes a certain picturesque quality.

🗺 K5 ✉ 28 rue des Blancs Manteaux, 75004 ☎ 01 42 74 40 15 🕐 Tue–Sat lunch, dinner Ⓜ Rambuteau

LOCAL WINE

At the intersection of rue Saule and rue Saint-Vincent there is a small hillside of vines—a remnant of the former vineyards of the Butte Montmartre. During the wine harvest there is a very popular, colorful festival with plenty of tastings. For more information, visit fetedesvendanges demontmartre.com.

LES PAPILLES €–€€

lespapillesparis.fr

The authentic decor sets you up for a genuine bistro experience where you can choose from a daily set menu of French dishes made with market-fresh ingredients. There's also a wine and fine food store.

🗺 H8 ✉ 30 rue Gay-Lussac 75005 ☎ 01 43 25 20 79 🕐 Tue–Sat lunch, dinner Ⓜ RER Luxembourg

PASSAGE 53 €€–€€€

passage53.com

Shinishi Sato's tiny restaurant in Paris's oldest shopping arcade packs a culinary punch, combining French ingredients with a modern approach. Sato is the first Japanese chef in France to earn two Michelin stars. Reservation is recommended.

🗺 H3 ✉ 53 passage des Panoramas, 75002 ☎ 01 42 33 04 35 🕐 Tue–Sat lunch, dinner Ⓜ Grands Boulevards

LE PETIT SAINT-BENOÎT €

petit-st-benoit.com

This popular, inexpensive classic was once the haunt of writers; the decor has barely changed since the 1930s. The menu features a long list of French classics ranging from frogs legs to boeuf bourguignon.

🗺 G6 ✉ 4 rue Saint-Benoît, 75006 ☎ 01 42 60 27 92 🕐 Mon–Sat lunch, dinner Ⓜ Saint-Germain-des-Prés

EAT

Taillevent is renowned for good food

LA PETITE ARDOISE €–€€

restaurantlapetiteardoise.fr

Regarded as one of the most popular restaurants in Fontainebleau, La Petite Ardoise serves classic French dishes from a variety of regions in France. Diners can choose small or large plate servings.

🔢 Off map 📧 16 rue Montebello, 77300 Fontainebleau 📞 01 64 24 08 66 🕐 Tue–Sat lunch, dinner 🚇 Fontainebleau–Avon

PINK MAMMA €€

bigmammagroup.com

A fun and authentically styled trattoria spread over four floors, each with a different decor style. The menu is filled with Italian staples, with a few fashionable extras such as burritos. They also do great grilled meats.

🔢 G1 📧 20b rue de Douai, 75009 📞 09 83 55 94 52 🕐 Daily lunch and dinner (no reservations) 🚇 Pigalle

PRAMIL €–€€

pramil.fr

With a menu based on seasonal produce, Alain Pramil has built up a loyal customer base. The presentation is refined and all at prices that make this one of Paris's best bistros in this price range.

🔢 L4 📧 9 rue du Vertbois 📞 01 42 72 03 60 🕐 Tue–Sat lunch, dinner, Sun dinner 🚇 Arts et Métiers, Temple

LE PROGRÈS €–€€

This is the kind of café where you'd expect to see a character from the 2001 film *Amélie*, which was shot in the area. The staff provide expert service and the *plat du jour* is a draw for lunchtime crowds.

🔢 C2 📧 7 rue des Trois-Frères, 75018 📞 01 42 64 07 37 🕐 Daily 9am–2am 🚇 Abbesses

RESTAURANT FRENCHIE €€

frenchie-restaurant.com

This massively popular nouveau bistro is owned by Gregory Marchand, who worked with Jamie Oliver in London before returning to his native France. The menu is limited but the fusion dishes are superb. The only downside is that you'll need to reserve at least a month ahead to be sure of getting a table. Try Marchand's wine bar across the street if Frenchie is full.

🔢 J4 📧 5–6 rue du Nil, 75002 📞 01 40 39 96 19 🕐 Mon–Fri dinner, Thu–Fri lunch (reservations obligatory) 🚇 Sentier

ROSE BAKERY €–€€

Organic food is served in this English bakery and tea shop, owned by a Franco-British couple. It is also a popular place for Sunday brunch.

🔢 C3 📧 46 rue des Martyrs, 75009 📞 01 42 82 12 80 🕐 Daily 9–6 (menu items 11–5.30) 🚇 Pigalle, Notre-Dame-de-Lorette

SEB'ON €€

seb-on.com

One of the best in a bunch of modern bistros that have sprung up in the Montmartre area, Seb'on is a tiny place presided over by Sebastien Heloin. He serves a small and ever-changing daily menu of market-fresh dishes with suitably impressive results.

🚩 H1 ✉ 62 rue d'Orsel, 75018 🕐 01 42 59 74 32 🕐 Sun lunch, Wed–Sat dinner 🚇 Abbesses

SEPTIME €€

septime-charonne.fr

One of a new generation of fine dining restaurants in Paris, Septime has quickly built legions of loyal patrons, though you'll have to surrender yourself to chef Bertrand Grebaut's fixed menu for dinner (you'll be asked about any food allergies before you are served). Lunch offers a good value.

🚩 Off map ✉ 80 rue de Charonne, 75011 🕐 01 43 67 38 29 🕐 Mon dinner, Tue–Fri lunch, dinner 🚇 Charonne

TAILLEVENT €€€

taillevent.com

The cooking at this elegant restaurant features classical foundations with subtle modern leanings. Opened some 70 years ago, it steadily gained in popularity and is worthy of its fine reputation.

🚩 C2 ✉ 15 rue Lamennais, 75008 🕐 01 44 95 15 01 🕐 Mon–Fri lunch, dinner. Closed late Jul to mid-Aug 🚇 George V, Charles de Gaulle–Étoile

LA TOUR D'ARGENT €€€

latourdargent.com

Come to this historic fine dining restaurant in the Latin Quarter for its spectacular view, its extensive wine cellar and the exceptionally tasty duck. It is quite superb.

🚩 K7 ✉ 15–17 quai de la Tournelle, 75005 (facing Île Saint-Louis) 🕐 01 43 54 23 31 🕐 Tue–Sat lunch, dinner. Closed Aug 🚇 Pont-Marie, Cardinal Lemoine

LA TRUFFIÈRE €€€

la-truffiere.fr

As the name suggests, this Michelin-starred restaurant is the place to explore the particular taste of the truffle. Chef Christophe Poard arrived in 2016 to inject new energy into the menu, which has been well received. The wine list is extensive, so enjoy.

🚩 J8 ✉ 4 rue Blainville, 75005 🕐 01 46 33 29 82 🕐 Tue–Sat lunch and dinner, Sun–Mon lunch 🚇 Place Monge

ZE KITCHEN GALERIE €€

zekitchengalerie.fr

The inventive cuisine at this chic restaurant has been rewarded with a Michelin star. Chef William Ledeuil combines the tastes and textures of southeast Asia with French techniques to produce creative dishes using French-grown fresh produce.

🚩 H6 ✉ 4 rue des Grands-Augustins, 75006 🕐 01 44 32 00 32 🕐 Mon–Fri lunch, dinner 🚇 Odéon

---

PICNIC LUNCHES

If your taste is for a *déjeuner sur l'herbe* in Fontainebleau, the rue Grande grocery stores are perfect for picnic supplies. In Versailles, the Marché Notre-Dame is an excellent covered market (closed on Mondays) for stocking up on lunch items. When in Chantilly, allow yourself to be tempted by the bakeries, with their delicious cakes and pastries filled with lashings of the eponymous cream.

Sleep

With options ranging from the luxurious to simple budget hotels, Paris has accommodations to suit everyone. In this section establishments are listed alphabetically.

SLEEP

Introduction

The city's hotels have seen an overhaul in recent years. Boutique hotels have sprung up all over Paris, especially in the Marais. Hotels around the Louvre, Champs-Élysées and Opéra tend to be more expensive, while those in the Latin Quarter are often smaller and more affordable.

Finding a Good Deal

Some of the luxury hotels are out of another era. Their stated prices are high but discounts can be found online or through some travel agents. Paris is one of the rare European capitals where you can find a pleasant, affordable place to stay in a central part of the city. The Paris Tourist Office (▷ 167) has information. You can reserve rooms if you visit in person.

Helpful Tips

Prices often drop in July and August and rise in May, June, September and October, for the trade fairs. Check whether the price includes breakfast. If you are bringing or renting a car, ask whether parking is available and the cost.

Outer Limits

Chain hotels on the outskirts can be less expensive, but they lack character. You'll also have to spend more time taking the Métro.

APARTMENT LIVING

● To rent an apartment, options include the UK-based Apartment Service (tel 020 8944 1444 from the UK; 011 44 20 8944 1444 from the US, apartmentservice.com) and Home Rental Service at 120 avenue des Champs-Élysées, 75008 (tel 01 42 25 65 40, homerental.fr).

● For bed-and-breakfast, try France Lodge at 2 rue Meissonnier, 75017 (tel 01 56 33 85 80, francelodge.fr); Good Morning Paris, 43 rue Lacépède, 75005 (tel 01 47 07 28 29, goodmorningparis.fr); and Bed & Breakfast France, Bellenuoe, 85100 Les Sables D'Olonne (tel 09 60 09 86 49, bedbreak.com).

From top: Hotel rooms come in all styles; the lobby of Le Meurice; let someone else take the strain with your luggage; a junior suite at Le Meurice

SLEEP

Directory

Sleeping A–Z

PRICES

Prices are approximate and based on a double room for one night.

€€€	€251–€800
€€	€151–€250
€	€50–€150

1K €€–€€€

1K-paris.com

Sharp modern design, variable lighting effects and great attention to detail characterize this splendid boutique hotel. There are 43 rooms and 9 suites (some rooms have an interior courtyard view), a highly popular bar, a relaxing covered terrace as well as an in-house restaurant.

➕ M4 ✉ 13 boulevard du Temple, 75003 ☎ 01 42 71 20 00 🚇 Filles du Calvaire

THE FIVE HOTEL €€–€€€

thefivehotel.com

Luxurious touches point to a high standard of quality at this boutique hotel. There's no doubt that the rooms here are very small but what they lack in space, they make up for in style, with their clean lines and bold blocks of color.

➕ J9 ✉ 3 rue Flatters, 75005 ☎ 01 43 31 75 21 🚇 Gobelins

GRAND HÔTEL MALHER €–€€

grandhotelmalher.com

A long-standing Paris hotel, Grand Hôtel Malher has reinvented itself with a contemporary makeover but it continues to be reasonably priced for its central location. The quieter rooms at the back look out over a pretty rear courtyard.

🔲 L6 ✉ 5 rue Malher, 75004 ☎ 01 42 72 60 92 🚇 St. Paul

L'HÔTEL €€€

l-hotel.com

A Parisian legend, L'Hôtel is exuberantly elegant and intimate. Oscar Wilde stayed here, and celebrities can often be found in the discreet bar. There are 20 individually styled rooms, some superbly appointed, as well as a hammam pool where guests can relax, and a restaurant.

🔲 G6 ✉ 13 rue des Beaux-Arts, 75006 ☎ 01 44 41 99 00 🚇 Saint-Germain-des-Prés

HÔTEL 29 LEPIC €€

29lepic.fr

This three-star hotel is near the Sacré-Cœur. Its simple but bright bedrooms have been carefully

furnished. There's free WiFi throughout and generous breakfast hours of 7am until 11am.

🔲 b2 ✉ 29 rue Lepic, 75018 ☎ 01 56 55 50 04 🚇 Blanche, Abbesses

HÔTEL DE L'ABBAYE €€€

hotelabbayeparis.com

This quaint, historic hotel was once a convent and now has a country house atmosphere. The lounge and most of the 40 rooms overlook a patio, and there's a cozy bar on site.

🔲 G7 ✉ 10 rue Cassette, 75006 ☎ 01 45 44 38 11 🚇 Saint-Sulpice

HÔTEL D'ANGLETERRE €€

hotel-dangleterre.com

This former 18th-century British embassy has a garden patio and individually appointed, spacious rooms with an elegant period feel. Ernest Hemingway lived in room 14 in 1921. There is a bar and a relaxing piano lounge.

🔲 G6 ✉ 44 rue Jacob, 75006 ☎ 01 42 60 34 72 🚇 Saint-Germain-des-Prés

HÔTEL DE L'AVRE €

hoteldelavre.com

This impeccably kept two-star hotel is justifiably popular with guests. The 25 individually decorated rooms vary in size and some look out over the rear courtyard. Breakfast is served in the pretty garden in spring and summer.

🔲 B8 ✉ 21 rue de l'Avre, 75015 ☎ 01 45 75 31 03 🚇 La Motte-Picquet–Grenelle

HOTEL CARON DE BEAUMARCHAIS €€

carondebeaumarchais.com

Set in a period townhouse styled to evoke the Age of

BUDGET HOTELS

Gone are the heady days when Paris was peppered with atmospheric basic hotels with their inimitable signs "eau à tous les étages" (water on every floor). Now there are usually bath or shower rooms with every bedroom, resulting in higher prices and smaller rooms.

So don't expect much space in budget hotel rooms, and be aware that breakfast may not be included. Receptionists usually speak a second language in hotels with two or more stars.

Enlightenment, the 19 rooms are compact but beautifully furnished in period style with sumptuous fabrics and elegant wallpapers used throughout. Lovers of clean minimalism should book elsewhere.

🔲 K6 ✉ 12 rue Vieille-du-Temple, 75004
☎ 01 42 72 34 12 🚇 St. Paul

HÔTEL DU COLLÈGE DE FRANCE €–€€

hotel-collegedefrance.com
This inexpensive family-owned hotel is set behind a Haussman-designed facade. There are 29 well-presented simple but modern rooms that vary in size. All are en suite; some have small balconies overlooking the street.

🔲 J7 ✉ 7 rue Thénard, 75005 ☎ 01 43 26 78 36 🚇 Maubert–Mutualité

HOTEL CRAYON €€

hotelcrayon.com
The creation of artist Julie Gauthron, this boutique hotel has individually styled rooms filled with items chosen by Julie herself. It is a contemporary space and some of the rooms are in-your-face bright; check the website before booking.

🔲 H4 ✉ 25 rue du Bouloi, 75001
☎ 01 42 36 54 19 🚇 Louvre–Rivoli, Les Halles

HÔTEL DESIGN DE LA SORBONNE €€–€€€

hotelsorbonne.com
This hotel has contemporary living down to a fine art. Each floor has photos, engravings and literary quotes that complement the British-style decor. The 38 bedrooms have iMac computers, among the lavish facilities.

🔲 H8 ✉ 6 rue Victor-Cousin, 75005
☎ 01 43 54 58 08 🚇 Cluny–La Sorbonne

HÔTEL DUC DE SAINT-SIMON €€

hotelducdesaintsimon.com
This elegant 18th-century town-house has been transformed into a small hotel with delightful period styling. It is pricey (at the top end of mid-range) but the antiques and setting, just off boulevard Saint-Germain, justify this. There are 34 comfortable rooms.

🔲 F6 ✉ 14 rue Saint-Simon, 75007
☎ 01 44 39 20 20 🚇 Rue du Bac

HOTEL EIFFEL TURENNE €€

hoteleiffelturenne.com
The bright and cozy rooms of this two-star hotel are comfortably furnished, but don't expect anything very spacious. Some rooms have views of the Eiffel Tower, which is only a short stroll away through the Champ de Mars. There's a small hotel bar.

🔲 D6 ✉ 20 avenue de Tourville, 75007
☎ 01 47 05 99 92 🚇 École Militaire

HÔTEL DU JEU DE PAUME €€€

jeudepaumehotel.com
This small, delightful hotel is carved out of a 17th-century royal tennis court. The interior is a surprise considering the age of the buildings, with many contemporary touches. There are 27 tasteful rooms and two large apartments for longer rentals.

🔲 K7 ✉ 54 rue Saint-Louis-en-l'Île, 75004
☎ 01 43 26 14 18 🚇 Pont Marie

JULES ET JIM €€

hoteljulesetjim.com
Three town houses come together in a contemporary ensemble that's

named after a Francois Truffaut film. The public spaces double as a photographic gallery. Rooms come in different styles and sizes, but they are all well furnished. The bar is a popular locale for events, and there's also an outside courtyard to enjoy in summer.

➕ K4 ✉ 11 rue des Gravilliers, 75003 ☎ 01 44 54 13 13 🚇 Arts et Metiers

HÔTEL DES MARRONNIERS €€

hoteldesmarronniers.com

The oak-beamed rooms and vaulted cellars here have been converted into relaxing lounges. There are 37 well-appointed and comfortable guest rooms; request one with a view of the garden. The hotel also boasts a lovely *salon du thé*.

➕ G6 ✉ 21 rue Jacob, 75006 ☎ 01 43 25 30 60 🚇 Saint-Germain-des-Prés

HÔTEL MOLIÈRE €€

hotel-moliere.fr

A small boutique hotel, the Molière has calm zen-like interiors. There are 32 rooms, one with a good-sized balcony. The bathrooms are tiny but contemporary. There's a sauna/wellness/fitness center on site, but no restaurant.

➕ G4 ✉ 21 rue Molière, 75001 ☎ 01 42 96 22 01 🚇 Pyramides, Palais-Royal

HÔTEL DES NATIONS SAINT-GERMAIN €–€€

paris-hotel-des-nations-st-germain.com

A modern hotel with contemporary decoration and delightful style touches, this small hotel has compact but well-equipped rooms. There is also an honesty bar here, and free Wi-Fi is available in all the rooms.

➕ K8 ✉ 54 rue Monge, 75005 ☎ 01 43 26 45 24 🚇 Cardinal Lemoine

HÔTEL LA PERLE €€

hotel-paris-laperle.com

This renovated 17th-century building on a quiet street has 38 rooms. It lies at the upper end of the mid-range price bracket, but the attention to detail, room decor and spacious communal areas are well worth the price. The large veranda is a charming setting for evening drinks and there's also a fitness room.

➕ G7 ✉ 14 rue des Canettes, 75006 ☎ 01 43 29 10 10 🚇 Mabillon

HÔTEL DE LA PLACE DES VOSGES €

hotelplacedesvosges.com

This 17th-century town house in the Marais offers minimalist styling, mixing period furniture and architectural details with stark white walls. Some of the 16 rooms overlook the courtyard.

➕ M6 ✉ 12 rue de Birague, 75004 ☎ 01 42 72 60 46 🚇 Bastille, Saint-Paul

HÔTEL SAINTE-BEUVE €€–€€€

hotelsaintebeuve.com

Between Montparnasse and the Luxembourg gardens, this exclusive hotel features a stylish blend of period antiques and modern furnishings. It has the atmosphere of a private club. Standard rooms are small, but there are connecting rooms to cater for families.

🔢 G8 ✉ 9 rue Sainte-Beuve, 75006 ☎ 01 45 48 20 07 🚇 Notre-Dame-des-Champs

HÔTEL SAN RÉGIS €€€

hotel-sanregis.fr

Popular with showbiz folk, this elaborately decorated hotel has 32 rooms and 11 suites. Interior designer Pierre-Yves Rochon mixes antique pieces with ornate chintz to re-create classic French Empire style. It's certainly exclusive, with prices to match.

🔢 D4 ✉ 12 rue Jean-Goujon, 75008 ☎ 01 44 95 16 16 🚇 Franklin D Roosevelt, Champs-Élysées–Clémenceau

HÔTEL DE L'UNIVERSITÉ €€

universitehotel.com

This Left Bank hotel *par excellence* has 27 rooms, some complete with (nonworking) fireplaces, antique furnishings and exposed beams. The pastel decor in the rooms and communal areas offers a calming refuge from city hustle and bustle after a busy day of sightseeing.

🔢 G6 ✉ 22 rue de l'Université, 75007 ☎ 01 42 61 09 39 🚇 Rue du Bac

LE MEURICE €€€

dorchestercollection.com

Situated just across the street from the Louvre, this historic 18th-century hotel has been thoroughly modernized, but the luxurious furnishings in the 160 rooms have more than a touch of Louis XVI style and elegance about them. French master-chef Alain Ducasse stamps his inimitable mark on the dining experience here.

🔢 F5 ✉ 228 rue de Rivoli, 75001 ☎ 01 44 58 10 10 🚇 Concorde, Tuileries

PAVILLON DE LA REINE €€€

pavillon-de-la-reine.com

Period decoration and lavish furnishings in this 17th-century building are enhanced by the peaceful and leafy garden. There are 54 rooms and suites. The hotel has a small spa but it does not have a restaurant.

🔢 M6 ✉ 28 place des Vosges, 75003 ☎ 01 40 29 19 19 🚇 Bastille, Chemin Vert

LES RIVES DE NOTRE-DAME €€–€€€

rivesdenotredame.com

Overlooking the banks of the Seine, this hotel has beamed ceilings, marble tiling, tapestries and fine wrought-iron furniture. It's a small property of only 10 rooms, so you are guaranteed an intimate atmosphere and a warm welcome. There are wonderful views of the river and also to Notre-Dame from some of the rooms.

🔢 J7 ✉ 15 quai Saint-Michel, 75005 ☎ 01 43 54 81 16 🚇 Saint-Michel

SLEEP

Need to Know

This section takes you through all the practical aspects of your trip to make it run more smoothly and to give you confidence before you go and while you are there.

NEED TO KNOW

Planning Ahead

WHEN TO GO

Spring is popular, when the chestnut trees are in blossom. The city reaches peak tourist capacity in hot, sunny July. However, with the Parisian exodus to the countryside in August the city is emptier than usual. Autumn is busy with trade fairs and rooms can be scarce and expensive.

TEMPERATURE

JAN	FEB	MAR	APR	MAY	JUN	JUL	AUG	SEP	OCT	NOV	DEC
6°C	7°C	12°C	16°C	20°C	23°C	25°C	26°C	21°C	16°C	10°C	7°C
43°F	45°F	54°F	61°F	68°F	73°F	77°F	79°F	70°F	61°F	50°F	45°F

Spring (April, May) takes time to get going. Things don't usually warm up until mid-May.
Summer (June to August) can be glorious. Days are longest in June, with the most sunshine and a pleasant temperature. It is usually hot and sunny in July, and often hot, humid and stormy in August.
Autumn (September to November) has crisp days and usually clear skies.
Winter (December to March) is rarely below freezing but it rains frequently, sometimes with hail, in January and March.

WHAT'S ON

January/February *Chinese New Year:* In Chinatown, 13th *arrondissement.*
April/May *International Paris Fair:* Consumer heaven at Porte de Versailles, foire deparis.fr.
Paris marathon: Starts from the Champs-Élysées, schneiderelectric parismarathon.com.
May *Labor Day* (1 May): Parades and symbolic lily-of-the-valley bouquets.
La Nuit des Musées: On one Saturday evening museums fling their doors open with music, drama and readings.
June *Paris Jazz Festival* (mid-Jun to Jul): Weekends

at Parc Floral de Paris (parisjazzfestival.fr).
Fête de la Musique (21 Jun): Music on the streets.
La Marche des Fiertés LGBT de Paris (Gay Pride) (Sat in late Jun): Popular procession, plus partying in the Marais district.
July *Bastille Day* (14 Jul): The most important French festival celebrates the 1789 storming of the Bastille. Fireworks and street dances on the evening of the 13th and a parade on the 14th on the Champs-Élysées.
July–August *Festival Paris l'Été:* Outdoor perfor-mances, quartierdete.com.
Paris Plages: Beaches

along the quays of the Seine.
September *Festival d'Automne à Paris* (mid-Sep to Dec): Music, theater and dance all over the city, festival-automne.com.
October *Foire Internationale d'Art Contemporain:* Paris's biggest modern art fair, fiac.com.
Nuit Blanche: For one night various cultural venues open all night, free.
November *Beaujolais Nouveau* (third Thu in Nov): Drinking in all the city's bars.
December *Paris International Boat Show* salonnautiqueparis.com.

PARIS ONLINE

visitparisregion.com
The website of the Paris Île de France regional
tourist authority has a huge quantity and variety
of information on Paris and the surrounding
region, including entertainment and events,
shopping, sport and leisure, children's Paris,
accommodations and public transportation.
It now has a new site dedicated to English-
language speakers.

parisinfo.com
The Paris Tourist Office online has listings and
practical information, sightseeing and links to
other useful sites covering every aspect of
leisure in the city. It also provides an online
hotel booking service.

parisbymouth.com
Information for foodies, or someone looking
for the latest hot bistro, rising star chef or up-
coming food festivals in the city.

parisvoice.com
Intended for English-speaking Parisians, this
site gives an insider's view of the city, with
features, events information, restaurant reviews,
classified ads, a Q&A column (dealing with
some very serious issues) and more.

paris.fr
The official site of Paris's mayor and city council
has information on museums, theaters, parks
and sport, as well as a virtual tour of the Hôtel
de Ville. There is also a wealth of civic news
aimed at Paris residents.

france.fr
The official website for the French tourist
authority has information for the whole of
France, but Paris features heavily. Find the
latest exhibition and concert information, plus
practical information about your stay in France.

paris-update.com
What's happening, updated weekly: art shows,
films, restaurants, concerts.

TRAVEL SITES

parisdigest.com
Independent guide showing
you around the city with
mainstream practical
information. A good range
of hotel, restaurant and
shopping guides.

fodors.com
A complete travel-planning
site. You can research
prices; book air tickets, cars
and rooms; ask questions
(and get answers) from
fellow travelers; and find
links to other sites.

PARIS WIFI

There is free access to WiFi
in almost 300 parks,
libraries and public
buildings in Paris. Hot spots
are shown with distinctive
oval signs. You'll need to
link to PARIS_WI-FI_ page,
select your pass, create a
password, fill in a form and
agree to terms. Each free
session lasts up to 2 hours.

Getting There

GETTING YOUR BEARINGS

Think of Paris as a snail, with its shell curling around the 1st *arrondissement* (district) right in the middle. The numbers of the other *arrondissements* follow clockwise, ending with the 20th on the eastern side of the city. *C'est logique, non?*

AIRPORTS

Most international flights arrive at Roissy Charles de Gaulle airport, with some international and French domestic flights arriving at Orly airport. Paris has good rail connections, including the Eurostar train direct from London.

60km (40 miles)

Roissy Charles de Gaulle Airport
Bus 50 mins, €17
Train 35 min, €10,30

Orly Airport
Bus 30 min, €12.50

FROM ROISSY CHARLES DE GAULLE

Roissy (tel 3950, outside France 331 70 36 39 50, adp.fr) is 23km (14 miles) northeast of central Paris and has three terminals. Air France currently operates out of Terminal 2. There are three ways to get to the city.

By bus: Le Bus Direct (lebusdirect.com) operates a bus service (Line 4) between the airport and Montparnasse and Gare de Lyon, every 30 minutes 6am–10pm (€17), and to the Arc de Triomphe (Étoile) and Porte Maillot (Line 2) every 20–30 minutes, 5.45am–11pm (€17). You can buy tickets from the driver (€1 extra) or at the Air France offices in the terminal. Or take the 50-minute trip on Roissybus that runs every 15 or 20 minutes from Terminals 1, 2 and 3 to Opéra, 6am–12.30am (€12).

By train: The RER (Réseau Express Régional) Line B takes around 35 minutes to reach central Paris (€10,30). Trains leave every 10–15 minutes.

By taxi: There are fixed rate fares between the airport and the downtown core. Fares are €50 to destinations on the left bank of the River Seine and €55 to destinations on the right bank. There's a €4 reservation fee (€7 if booked in advance) or a €2.60 pick up fee.

FROM ORLY

Orly (tel 3950, outside France 331 70 36 39 50, adp.fr), the smaller of Paris's two main international airports, is 14km (8.5 miles) from central Paris with no direct train to the city.

By bus: Le Bus Direct provides shuttle buses to Les Invalides, Étoile and Gare Montparnasse every 20–30 minutes, 5.50am–11.30pm (€12.50). The trip takes about 30 minutes.

By train: The Orlyval train, which operates daily 6am–11.35pm, will take you to Antony, where you can change for Line B of the RER rail system (€12.05). From here, it's around 25 minutes to central Paris.

By taxi: A taxi costs €30 to destinations on the left bank of the River Seine and €35 to destinations on the right bank and takes 15–30 minutes.

EUROSTAR

The Eurostar (tel 01 70 70 60 88 in France, 03432 186 186 in the UK, eurostar.com) takes you from London to the Gare du Nord in the heart of Paris in about 2 hours 15 minutes. From here, there are good Métro and RER connections, or you can take a taxi.

THALYS

Thalys (tel 0825 84 25 97, thalys.com) offers daily high-speed train services linking Paris to Brussels, Antwerp, Amsterdam, Cologne and Dortmund.

BUDGET OPTIONS

Within Europe, low-cost airlines such as easyJet (easyjet.com) and Ryanair (ryanair.com) offer some attractive and competitive prices that can sometimes beat the cost of traveling by train. But the tickets are not always bargains; they are priced according to availability and demand. It is usually best to book as far in advance as possible. Keep in mind that Ryanair flies in and out of Beauvais airport, 70km (43 miles) from Paris, so the low cost of a ticket may not be worth the time lost in traveling to and from the airport. EasyJet uses Roissy Charles de Gaulle airport for flights from the UK.

VISAS AND TRAVEL INSURANCE

Visas are not required for EU, US or Canadian nationals, but you will need a valid passport. (Check the latest requirements before you travel.) EU citizens receive reduced-cost medical treatment with the European Health Insurance Card (EHIC). Full insurance is still strongly advised and is essential for all other travelers.

Getting Around

Paris has a mixed record on
access and amenities. On
the Métro, only the Meteor
line (No. 14) has easy access
for people with disabilities.
Since 2009, all bus lines in
the city are wheelchair
accessible and 80 percent of
the bus stops have been
specially adapted. Infomobi
(☎ 09 70 81 83 85,
infomobi.com) is a service
with information and news
about public transportation
for visitors with a disability.
RATP's Les Compagnons du
Voyage (☎ 01 58 76 08 33,
compagnons.com) provides
companions for visitors with
disabilities (if not in an
electric wheelchair), but for
a fee. Two taxi companies,
G7 (☎ 01 41 27 66 99,
taxisg7.com) and Taxis
PMR (☎ 06 12 68 27 60,
taxipmr.onlc.fr), will take
wheelchairs. The website
of the Paris Tourist Office
(parisinfo.com) has
information for visitors with
disabilities, including a list
of the city's accessible sights.
The downloadable
Accessible Paris guide has
more information about
getting around, and can be
accessed on the Paris Tourist
Office website.

MÉTRO

The best way to travel around Paris is by Métro
or RER, two separate but linked systems
(ratp.fr). The RER is the suburban line, which
passes through the heart of the city. The Métro
is the underground system, with 14 main lines
and 303 stations. Both are inexpensive and effi-
cient, and free maps of all the routes are
available at station ticket windows. Any place is
within easy walking distance of a Métro or RER
station. Both systems function in the same way
and the tickets are interchangeable within the
city. It is cheaper to buy a *carnet* of 10 tickets
than to buy each ticket separately.

● Métro lines are always identified by their
destination and a number; connections are
shown in *correspondances* panels displayed
on the platform.

● The first Métros run at 5.30am, and the last
around 1.15am (2.15am Fri and Sat).

● Keep your ticket until you exit—it has to be
re-inserted on the RER, and ticket inspectors
prowl the Métro.

TICKETS AND PASSES

● Tickets and passes function for Métro, buses,
trams and RER.

● One ticket (€1.90) gives access to zones 1
and 2 of the Métro network, the RER within
Paris, trams and Parisian and suburban buses.
A *carnet* of 10 tickets is €14.50.

● Single tickets (known as Ticket t+) are only
valid for a single journey without changing
between bus, Métro, tram and RER.

● Prices of passes and suburban RER tickets
depend on how many travel zones you intend
to pass through.

● Mobilis is a one-day pass, valid on the Métro,
buses and RER.

● A Paris Visite card gives unlimited travel for
one, two, three or five days plus discounts at
certain monuments, but you need to do a lot
of traveling to make it pay.

● *Navigo Découverte* travel cards for visitors
are obtainable from stations and valid for a
week *(Forfait Navigo Semaine)*, starting
Monday and ending the following Sunday,

or month *(Forfait Navigo Mois)*. Both are valid on routes from the airports to downtown. You'll need a passport photo and the card itself costs €7.60.

BATOBUS
Traveling by Batobus—a river shuttle boat—is fun (late-Apr to early Sep daily 10–9.30, every 25 minutes; late-Mar to late-Apr and early Sep to early Nov, daily 10–7, every 20 minutes; early-Nov to late-Mar Mon–Thu 10–5, every 40 minutes, Fri–Sun 10–7, every 40 minutes). It stops at the Eiffel Tower, Musée d'Orsay, Saint-Germain-des-Prés, Notre-Dame, Jardin des Plantes, Hôtel de Ville, Louvre, Champs-Élysées and Beaugrenelle. You can join at any point. An all-day ticket costs €17, a two-day ticket costs €19 (tel 01 76 64 79 12, batobus.com).

BICYCLES
Bicycles are available at self-service stations across Paris, as part of the Vélib' hire scheme (tel 01 30 79 79 30, velib.paris.fr). One-day (€1.70) or seven-day (€8) tickets are available; major cards are accepted.

TAXIS
Taxis can be hailed in the street if the roof sign is illuminated or can be found at taxi ranks outside most main attractions. There are three tariffs in central Paris: A applies Mon–Sat 10am–5pm; B applies Mon–Sat 5pm–10am, Sun 7am–midnight and 24 hours on public holidays Mon–Sat; C applies Sun midnight–7am. There are extra charges for the fourth and fifth passengers. Tip drivers 10 percent.
● The initial fee for hiring a taxi is €4 if booked immediately, €7 if prebooked, or there's a €3.83 pick up fee and the minimum fare is €7. Tariff A is €1.06 per km, B €1.29 and C €1.56. If luggage is more than 5kg (11 lbs) there is an excess of €1.
● Taxi ranks that have telephones can be called on 01 45 30 30 30. Select your *arrondissement* with the help of the voice server, who will connect you to the closest rank.

STUDENT VISITORS
● An International Student Identity Card can reduce cinema charges, entrance fees to museums and air and rail travel.
● MIJE (Maison Internationale de la Jeunesse et des Étudiants)
✉ 6 rue Fourcy, 75004
☎ 01 42 74 23 45, mije.com
Ⓜ Saint-Paul
🕐 Daily 7am–1am. Three hostels for young people in the heart of Paris.
● CIDJ (Centre d'Information et de Documentation Jeunesse)
✉ 101 quai Branly, 75015
☎ 01 44 49 12 00, cidj.com
Ⓜ Bir-Hakeim
🕐 Tue–Fri 1–6, Sat 1–5. Youth information office for jobs, courses, sport.

TOURIST OFFICE
● Office du Tourisme de Paris
✉ 25 rue des Pyramides, 75001
☎ parisinfo.com
🕐 Nov–Apr daily 9–7; May–Oct 10–7 (Sun from 11)
Ⓜ Pyramides
❓ There are English-speaking staff in the office

Essential Facts

MONEY

The euro is the official currency of France. There are bank notes in denominations of 5, 10, 20, 50, 100, 200 and 500 euros and coins in denominations of 1, 2, 5, 10, 20 and 50 cents and 1 and 2 euros.

TIPPING

In every restaurant, by law, a 15 percent service charge and all relevant taxes are already in the prices on the menu. If the service was especially pleasant, or if you feel odd about leaving nothing, then you can leave another couple of euros or 5 percent. In taxis, it is customary to give the driver a 10 percent tip, but only if you are happy with the service.

CREDIT CARDS

● Credit cards are widely accepted.
● VISA cards are the most widely accepted and can be used in cash dispensers. Make sure you know your international PIN. MasterCard and Diners Club are also widely accepted.
● American Express is less common, so Amex cardholders requiring cash should look out for cash dispensers at post offices or check the information on the website americanexpress. com for other locations.

ETIQUETTE

● Shake hands on introduction and on leaving; once you know people well replace this with a peck on both cheeks.
● Always use *vous* unless the other person breaks into *tu*.
● It is polite to add *Monsieur, Madame* or *Mademoiselle* when addressing strangers.
● Always say *bonjour* and *au revoir* in shops.
● When calling waiters, use *Monsieur* or *Madame* (not *garçon*).
● Dress carefully. More emphasis is put on appearance in France than in other countries. Smart casual dress is the norm.

FOREIGN EXCHANGE

● Only banks with Change signs will change foreign currency/traveler's checks; a passport is necessary for identification. Bureaux de change are open longer hours but rates can be poorer. Fees for cashing euro traveler's checks can be high.
● Airport and station exchange desks are open daily 6 or 6.30am to 10 or 10.30pm.

MEDICINES AND MEDICAL TREATMENT

● Minor ailments can often be treated at pharmacies.
● Public hospitals have a 24-hour emergency service *(urgences)* and specialist doctors. Payment is made on the spot, but if you are hospitalized see the *assistante sociale* to arrange payment through your insurance.
● House calls are made by SOS Médecins, tel 36 24 or 01 47 07 77 77, sosmedecins.fr.

● For dental problems, contact SOS Dentaire, tel 01 43 37 51 00, sos-dentaire.com.
● 24-hour pharmacy: Pharmacie Malesherbes, 84 avenue des Champs-Élysées, 75008, tel 01 45 62 02 41.
● Publicis drugstore (133 avenue des Champs-Élysées, tel 01 44 43 75 07) is a pharmacy, café, newsagent and tobacconist, open until 2am. With a night pharmacy open 2am–8am.
● Pharmacies display a green cross outside.

NATIONAL HOLIDAYS
● 1 January, Easter Monday, 1 May, 8 May, Ascension (a Thursday in May), Whit Monday (late May or early June), 14 July, 15 August, 1 November, 11 November, 25 December.
● Sunday services for public transportation operate; many local shops, restaurants and even some large stores remain open on national holidays.

POST OFFICES
● Stamps can be bought at *tabacs*; post mail in any yellow mailbox.
● All post offices offer express courier post (Chronopost), and photocopy machines.

PUBLIC TOILETS
● Public toilets are free and generally well maintained, although they are not plentiful.
● The Point WCs, on the Champs-Élysées, at the Carrousel du Louvre, Metro Cluny–La Sorbonne, and on boulevard Haussmann are "super loos," for €1.50.
● Malls and department stores have good public facilities and every café has a toilet, but order a drink too.

EMERGENCY NUMBERS
● Crisis-line in English: SOS Help ☎ 01 46 21 46 46 soshelpline.org
🕐 3pm–11pm
● Police ☎ 17
● Any emergency ☎ 112
● Ambulance (SAMU) ☎ 15
● Fire (*sapeurs pompiers*) ☎ 18
● Anti-poison ☎ 01 40 05 48 48
● Police lost-property office ✉ 36 rue des Morillons, 75015 ☎ 08 21 00 25 25

ELECTRICITY
● Voltage is 220V; French sockets take plugs with two round pins.

EMBASSIES/CONSULATES

US Embassy	✉ 2 avenue Gabriel, 75008	☎ 01 43 12 22 22
US Consulate	✉ 4 avenue Gabriel, 75008	☎ 01 43 12 22 22
Canadian Embassy	✉ 35 avenue Montaigne, 75008	☎ 01 44 43 29 00
British Embassy	✉ 35 rue du Faubourg Saint-Honoré, 75008	☎ 01 44 51 31 00
British Consulate	✉ 16 rue d'Anjou, 75008	☎ 01 44 51 31 00
Australian Embassy	✉ 4 rue Jean-Rey, 75015	☎ 01 40 59 33 00
New Zealand Embassy	✉ 103 rue de Grenelle, 75007	☎ 01 45 01 43 43

OPENING HOURS

- Banks: Mon–Fri 9–12.30, 2–5. Closed on public holidays and often the preceding afternoon.
- Post offices: Mon–Fri 8–7, Sat 8–12. The main post office (✉ 52 rue du Louvre, 75001) is closed for renovations until 2018.
- Shops: Mon–Sat 9–7 or 10–8. Some close Mon and an hour at lunch.
- Museums: National museums close on Tue, municipal museums on Mon. Individual opening hours vary.

PRESS

- Main dailies are *Le Monde* (serious, centrist), *Libération* (left-wing) and *Le Figaro* (right-wing).
- For weekly listings of cultural events, buy a copy of *Pariscope* (pariscope.fr; the most popular listings magazine) or *L'Officiel des Spectacles* (offi.fr).
- Central newspaper kiosks and newsagents stock European dailies (widely available on the day of issue) and *USA Today*.
- Visit trouverlapresse.com to find out exactly where you can buy your favorite publication.

SENSIBLE PRECAUTIONS

- Watch wallets and purses as pickpockets are active, particularly in busy bars, flea markets, cinemas, the Métro, railroad stations and the airport.
- Ticket touts operate at train and Métro stations. Buy from machines or ticket kiosks.
- Keep the numbers of your traveler's checks separate from the checks.
- It is important to make a declaration at a local *commissariat* (police station) to claim losses on your insurance.
- Women are generally safe traveling alone or together, although the same risks apply as in any city in western Europe. Deal with any unwanted attention firmly and politely. Avoid the Métro late at night.

TELEPHONES

- Most phone booths use Orange cards (*télécarte* for 50 or 120 units), sold at post offices, *tabacs* or main Métro stations.
- To call France from the US, dial 011 33, then leave out the first zero. To call the US from France dial 00 1, followed by the number.
- To call France from the UK, dial 00 33—omit the first zero from the number. To call the UK from France, dial 00 44—omit the first zero.
- All numbers in the Île-de-France, including Paris, start with 01 unless they are premium rate, when they start with 08; some are toll-free.
- Numbers in the French provinces begin with: 02 Northwest, 03 Northeast, 04 Southeast, 05 Southwest.

TICKETS

- The Paris Museum Pass (parismuseum pass.fr) gives access to 59 museums and monuments. It is valid for two, four or six consecutive days. You can buy it online or at tourist offices, museums and Fnac stores.
- Paris Passlib' is available from tourist offices across Paris. It offers entry to over 50 museums and monuments plus reductions at other attractions, a river cruise, Big Bus tour and all public transportation costs for a period of two, three, or five consecutive days.

Words and Phrases

BASIC VOCABULARY

oui/non	yes/no
s'il vous plaît	please
merci	thank you
excusez-moi	excuse me
pardon	I'm sorry
bonjour	hello, good morning
bonsoir	good evening
au revoir	goodbye
de rien/avec plaisir	you're welcome
parlez-vous anglais?	do you speak English?
je ne comprends pas	I don't understand
combien?	how much?
trop cher	too expensive
je voudrais...	I'd like...
où est/sont...?	where is/are...?
ici/là	here/there
tournez à gauche/droite	turn left/right
tout droit	straight on
quand?	when?
aujourd'hui	today
hier	yesterday
demain	tomorrow
combien de temps?	how long?
à quelle heure?	at what time?
à quelle heure ouvrez/fermez-vous?	what time do you open/close?
avez-vous...?	do you have...?
une chambre simple	a single room
une chambre double	a double room
avec/sans salle de bains	with/without bathroom
le petit déjeuner	breakfast
le déjeuner	lunch
le dîner	dinner
c'est combien?	how much is this?
puis-je réserver une table	I'd like to book a table
une bouteille/un verre de...	a bottle/glass of...
acceptez-vous des cartes de crédit?	do you take credit cards?
j'ai besoin d'un médecin/dentiste	I need a doctor/dentist
pouvez-vous m'aider?	can you help me?
où est l'hôpital?	where is the hospital?
où est le commissariat?	where is the police station?

NUMBERS

un	1
deux	2
trois	3
quatre	4
cinq	5
six	6
sept	7
huit	8
neuf	9
dix	10
onze	11
douze	12
treize	13
quatorze	14
quinze	15
seize	16
dix-sept	17
dix-huit	18
dix-neuf	19
vingt	20
vingt-et-un	21
trente	30
quarante	40
cinquante	50
soixante	60
soixante-dix	70
quatre-vingts	80
quatre-vingt-dix	90
cent	100
mille	1,000

MONTHS

janvier	January
février	February
mars	March
avril	April
mai	May
juin	June
juillet	July
août	August
septembre	September
octobre	October
novembre	November
décembre	December

Index

We would like to thank the following photographers, companies and picture libraries for their assistance in the preparation of this book.

2i Paris Tourist Office/Marc Bertrand; 2ii, 2iii AA/K Blackwell; 2iv Hemis/Alamy; 2v AA/ M Jourdan; 3i, 3ii, 3iii, 3iv, 4 AA/K Blackwell; 5 Paris Tourist Office/Marc Bertrand; 6/7t AA/K Blackwell; 6/7ct PARAMOUNT/THE KOBAL COLLECTION; 6/7cb THE KOBAL COLLECTION; 6/7b Kristjan Porm/Alamy; 7ct AA/K Blackwell; 7cb MGM/THE KOBAL COLLECTION; 8/9t, 8c AA/K Blackwell; 8/9b AA/K Paterson; 9ct AA/K Blackwell; 9cb © Paris Tourist Office – Photographer Amélie Dupont; 10l AA/K Blackwell; 10r The Bridgeman Art Library; 11 Keystone/Getty Images; 12, 14, 15tl, 15cl, 15tr, 15cr AA/K Blackwell; 16l Centre Pompidou; 16tr AA/T Souter; 16/17 Susana Vázquez; 17l AA/C Sawyer; 17tr Susana Vázquez; 17cr Centre Pompidou; 18t, 18b, 18tl, 19cl, 19r, 20l, 20/21t, 20c, 21c AA/K Blackwell; 21r AA/M Jourdan; 22t, 22cl, 22cr, 23t, 23c AA/K Blackwell; 24l AA/M Jourdan; 24tr AA; 24cr, 25tl, 25cl, 25r AA/K Blackwell; 26/27 age fotostock/Alamy; 27tr AA/C Sawyer; 27cr, 28l AA/K Blackwell; 28/29t GAUTIER Stephane/SAGAPHOTO.COM/Alamy Stock Photo; 28/29tc, 29t, 29c AA/K Blackwell; 30 AA/C Sawyer; 30/31t AA/K Paterson; 30/31c, 31t AA/M Jourdan; 31c AA/K Paterson; 32l, 32/33t AA/M Jourdan; 32/33c AA/J Tims; 33t The Bridgeman Art Library; 33c Susana Vázquez; 34 AA/J Tims; 35tl AA/K Blackwell; 35c Hemis/Alamy Stock Photo; 36, 36/37 AA/K Blackwell; 37t imageBROKER/Alamy; 37cr AA/K Blackwell; 38l AA/M Jourdan; 38/9t Danita Delimont/Alamy; 38/9b Paris Le Marais/Alamy; 39r AA/P Kenward; 40 AA/K Blackwell; 41tl Giraudon/The Bridgeman Art Library; 41cl The Art Archive/Alamy; 41r Hemis/Alamy; 42 AA/K Blackwell; 42/43t AA/M Jourdan; 42/43c AA/K Blackwell; 43t AA/B Rieger; 43cl, 43cr, 44, 45l AA/K Blackwell; 45r, 46/47, 47l AA/K Blackwell; 47r AA/M Jourdan; 48 AA/T Souter 48/49t AA/K Blackwell; 48/49c AA/K Paterson; 49, 50l, 50r, 50/51, 51l AA/K Blackwell; 51t AA/M Jourdan; 51c AA/K Blackwell; 52 AA/C Sawyer; 53l AA/P Kenward; 53t Paris Tourist Office/Marc Bertrand; 53c Andrew Duke/Alamy; 54l AA/K Blackwell; 54r Glenn Harper/Alamy; 54/55 Jon Arnold Images Ltd/ Alamy; 55 JOHN KELLERMAN/Alamy; 56, 56/57t, 56c, 57l AA/K Blackwell; 57tr, 57cr AA/J Tims; 58-59 RossHelen editorial/Alamy; 60, 60/61b, 60/61c, 61t, 61c, 62, 63tl AA/K Blackwell; 63c AA/M Jourdan; 63tc AA/K Blackwell; 63tr Hemis/Alamy; 64, 66l, 66r, 67l, 67r, 68 AA/K Blackwell; 69l AA/C Sawyer; 69r © Paris Tourist Office – Photographer Amélie Dupont; 70l, 70r AA/K Blackwell; 71l JOHN KELLERMAN/Alamy; 71r, 72 AA/K Blackwell; 73l AA/C Sawyer; 73r AA/M Jourdan; 74 Alexander Krassel/Alamy Stock Photo; 75l AA/C Sawyer; 75r, 76 AA/K Blackwell; 77l, 77r AA/D Noble; 78l Disney Enterprises, Inc; 78r Disney Enterprises, Inc; 79 AA/D Noble; 80 Hemis/Alamy; 82t AA/K Blackwell; 82b AA/J Tims; 83t, 83b, 86i AA/K Blackwell; 86ii imageBROKER/Alamy; 86iii AA/K Blackwell; 86iv AA/M Jourdan; 86v, 87 © Paris Tourist Office – Photographer Amélie Dupont; 88t Christophe Testi/Alamy; 88b, 89t AA/K Blackwell; 89b AA/C Sawyer; 92i, 92ii AA/K Blackwell; 92iii AA/K Paterson; 92iv, 92v, 92vi AA/K Blackwell; 94t, 94b AA/M Jourdan; 95 AA/K Blackwell; 98i Centre Pompidou; 98ii AA/K Blackwell; 98iii © Paris Tourist Office – Photographer – Agnès Moreau; 100, 101t, 101b, 104i, 104ii, 104iii AA/K Blackwell; 104iv AA/J Tims; 104v AA/K Blackwell; 104vi AA/M Jourdan 106t © Paris Tourist Office – Photographer Daniel Thierry; 106b AA/M Jourdan; 107t AA/J Tims; 107b AA/P Enticknap; 110t AA/T Souter; 110b AA/J Tims; 111l AA/K Blackwell; 111r, 112t AA/M Jourdan; 112c AA/K Blackwell; 112b AA/M Jourdan; 113t AA/K Blackwell; 113c © Paris Tourist Office – Photographer Marc Bertrand; 116i, 116ii, 116iii, 116iv, 117 AA/K Blackwell; 118 © Paris Tourist Office – Photographer Sarah Sargent; 120/121t Paris Tourist Office/Marc Bertrand; 120/121ct Paris Tourist Office/David Lefranc; 120cb, 120/121cb, 120/121b, 125 AA/C Sawyer; 127, 128, 130 AA/K Blackwell; 132/133t, 132ct Paris Tourist Office/ David Lefranc; 132/133ct AA/K Blackwell; 132/133cb Paris Tourist Office/Amélie Dupont; 133cb AA/P Enticknap; 132b AA/K Paterson; 133b, 140 AA/K Blackwell; 142i AA/ C Sawyer; 142ii, 142iii, 142iv, 144, 147, 148 AA/K Blackwell; 150 AA/C Sawyer; 152 AA/K Blackwell; 154i © Paris Tourist Office – Photographer Marc Bertrand; 154ii Courtesy of Dorchester Collection; 154iii AA/C Sawyer; 154iv Courtesy of Dorchester Collection; 160 AA/K Blackwell.

Every effort has been made to trace the copyright holders, and we apologize in advance for any unintentional omissions or errors. We would be pleased to apply any corrections in a following edition of this publication.

Paris 25 Best

WRITTEN BY Fiona Dunlop and Neville Walker
UPDATED BY Lindsay Bennett
SERIES EDITOR Clare Ashton
COVER DESIGN Jessica Gonzalez
DESIGN WORK Tom Whitlock and Liz Baldin
IMAGE RETOUCHING AND REPRO Ian Little

ISBN 978-1-6409-7217-9

FIFTEENTH EDITION

Printed and bound in China by 1010 Printing Group Limited

10 9 8 7 6 5 4 3 2 1

A05671
Maps in this title produced from mapping data supplied by Global Mapping, Brackley, UK © Global Mapping and data from openstreetmap.org
© OpenStreetMap contributors
Transport map © Communicarta Ltd, UK

Titles in the Series

- Amsterdam
- Bangkok
- Barcelona
- Berlin
- Boston
- Brussels and Bruges
- Budapest
- Chicago
- Dubai
- Dublin
- Edinburgh
- Florence
- Hong Kong
- Istanbul
- Krakow
- Las Vegas
- Lisbon
- London
- Madrid
- Melbourne
- Milan
- Montréal
- Munich
- New York City
- Orlando
- Paris
- Rome
- San Francisco
- Seattle
- Shanghai
- Singapore
- Sydney
- Tokyo
- Toronto
- Venice
- Vienna
- Washington, D.C.